THE NINE CYCLES
OF
A RICH LIFE

Success and happiness are about many things
But above all else, success and happiness are about timing –
Accurate Timing

Anna M. Belcastro
World Renaissance

Published by World Renaissance
Sydney, Australia.
Cover design by Box Car Graphics
Internal design by Publicious Book Publishing

Published with the assistance of
Publicious Book Publishing
www.publicious.com.au

Dedication

This book is dedicated to all who are willing to step up and say 'yes' to Life. To all who are willing to align themselves with Life, to meet Her and walk alongside Her, through the challenges, opportunities and triumphs. This book is dedicated to you.

Also by Anna M. Belcastro

FROM NOW TO ETERNITY
(Previously published as 2012 from here to eternity)

Contents

Introduction

The human mind is constantly searching for answers to life's complexities. If only we could go back to our yesteryears with the knowledge we have today. But life doesn't work like that – or does it? In reality it does and it doesn't. We cannot, as Cher sings, 'turn back time'. We cannot return to that place in time when we were young, equipped with the knowledge that our years of experience have given us. But, for sure, we can prepare ourselves to take advantage of the opportunities of our todays. For sure, we can prepare ourselves to take advantage of the opportunities to shape our tomorrows for a rich and meaningful life.

Life was never intended to be lived from a hit-or-miss perspective. Nor with a deterministic belief that we are powerless to change our lives. Success, happiness and wellbeing do not abide in the realm of luck, but more so in our knowledge, belief systems and, most decisively, in accurate timing. Once we have the knowledge and tools we need to live a rich life, what's left is for us to decide if we want it. The freedom to choose is ours. Through Universal and Personal Time Cycles, Life constantly offers us opportunities for growth – spiritually and materially. The choice to say yes or no to those opportunities, however, is ours to make. Sometimes we fail to see an opportunity. At other times we may deem it as requiring too much work, too much effort, so we retreat. And so we miss the chance to maximise success and happiness in our lives, either because we don't see it clearly, or because we can't be bothered putting in the effort needed to meet the requirements for their attainment.

It is my intention that the knowledge, wisdom and information within these pages will encourage you to see Life's opportunities more clearly, and so eliminate the temptation or inclination to miss them or side-step them. The privilege to choose, though, will still be yours. Will you say yes to that opportunity to take charge of your life, to take the lead, or will you tell yourself it's too hard? Will you take the opportunity to allow Life to guide and direct you, or will you insist on holding onto the controls, wanting things your way, until you lose out? Will you take the opportunity to grow your wealth portfolio or will you ignore it because it calls for a little more conscious choosing in your spending?

Most of life is lived in a hit-or-miss manner. If we continue to live life from this shaky base, not knowing what to expect, not knowing how to best respond, is it any wonder then that we see our lives as more of a struggle than a joy, more stressful than content? You can choose to respond to Life's opportunities confidently, with the knowledge to choose with love and wisdom, or you can continue on that hit or miss platform and simply hope that things will improve for you ... someday, somehow.

Life constantly returns the ball in your court. How will you play it? I encourage you to play it to win! I encourage you to always play a Life shot to win. Anything less would be self-sabotage of the worst kind and not worthy of the unique and talented person you were born to be and the rich and meaningful life which awaits your willingness to say 'yes'.

Part 1:

Towards A Rich Life

Consider a rich dessert. It is a work of art, a vision of beauty, which tantalises your taste buds before you even taste it. Once you savour the first mouthful, you discover to your delight that it is neither too sweet nor too tart. Nor is it gluttonous in quantity, but precisely enough to be pleasurably and delectably enjoyable. It is perfectly balanced. It does not war with your stomach but soothes it and is just enough of a good thing to complete your dining experience. It leaves you wanting more, yet you know that more would not enhance but might diminish what has been a most pleasurable and sensuous human experience.

Now, consider a rich life. It is in many ways like a rich dessert. The beauty of a rich life is that it radiates a good feeling about yourself and your place within the human family. It fills that part of you that is beyond only money. A rich life includes money, but being money rich is not its sole purpose. Money can be like a warm overcoat on a winter's day. It is a necessity as well as a want. Money is the difference between a hand-me-down coat or your coat of choice. And if we are to speak honestly, we would all prefer a coat of our choosing. Some people will tell you that money is 'the source of all evil'. But I do not believe this. Misers can be rich or poor. If you can handle little money then it's likely that you can also handle big money. If you are poor and generous

1

then you can be rich and generous. Don't be fooled. If you are a good person with little money, you can be a good person with much money. It rests with how you choose to exchange your money. What you choose to do with your money determines whether you are simply money rich or whether you live a rich life. The choice is yours to make and it's your choice which determines whether you will be a money-rich person with a poor life or a wealthy philanthropist living a rich life.

While for many it's money and wealth that come to mind when they hear the word 'rich,' a rich life includes more than money. A rich life must include more than money, otherwise one's life becomes lopsided and unbalanced, not unlike the Tower of Pisa. And so, I will tell you that in truth money is only a part of a rich life. Being money rich does not guarantee love, peace and joy. Then again, neither does being poor guarantee love, peace and joy. When you are money rich, you will be able to give to those in need or to a worthy project. But if you are money rich and lack a rich life, then you may well find giving more of a struggle than a joy, because when money is not coupled with a rich life, it remains connected to lack and struggle. The lack of giving because there might not be enough left for you. The struggle of the constant need to accumulate more and more, just in case. And this is because, though money may be plentiful, a richness of life is missing. The human in us longs for money richness while the spirit in us longs for a rich life. What many fail to understand is that a rich life does not deny money but welcomes it, accepts it, and marries it into the richness of life.

A rich life, therefore, is a life fulfilled, a life full of meaning. Above all a rich life is lived in love, peace and joy. It gives you a feeling of OK-ness like nothing else. It allows you to extend that love beyond your family circle to the outer community. The peace you feel allows you to extend that peace in the creation of richness not merely for loved ones, for those closest to you, but also for others beyond your family circle. All this without feeling lack in your own life. The joy you feel within you manifests in an optimistic view of others and of our world. It still allows you to see the ugliness, the injustices, but it protects you from becoming overwhelmed by it and from feeling a sense of uselessness to help better it. A rich life allows you to see life's beauty amidst its ugliness.

It's for many reasons that a rich life is to be encouraged and pursued for all it's worth, for all its promises and for its authentic and humbling power. Yes, a rich life is both humble and powerful. The authentic power of a rich life is *impastata* with humility. Humility is not a quality sought after in today's society and yet it forms an important part of authentic power, success, happiness and, of course, a rich and meaningful life. It is that quality which shouts gratitude from inside you, from your heart space and can enrich not only your life but also the lives of those around you.

You might think it impossible for you to have a rich life. That thought is understandable if you've never experienced it. I remember when I began learning to drive a car. I felt so uncoordinated and powerless to master all that it entailed. I thought I'd never be able to manage the clutch and accelerator to enable a smooth transition between the two. But I did. I could not have done it on my own though. If my brother had not chosen to give of his time so I could practise and had my driving instructor not chosen to share her skills teaching me, I doubt I would have learned to drive on my own. There's not much we can do without the generosity of others. If farmers didn't grow crops, we would not have any to buy. If it wasn't for milk-producing animals, we would have no milk, or cream, or cheese … Work becomes a generous sharing of our skills and talents in exchange for what we need and want, for building a rich life.

Some people have a tough time working for others. They don't like to see their employers making a profit. This comes from a mentality of lack and will railroad the way to money richness and a rich life. If you cannot handle someone else's success, Life reads it as you not being capable of handling your success either. Life operates on a give and receive momentum. When we forget this, things become lopsided and unstable. When we are aware of and keep in mind Life's momentum of giving and receiving, we are on our way towards a rich life. When you can be happy for another's success, for another's joy, then yours is already in the field of creation. I believe the fastest way to get what you want is to genuinely want it for others just as much as you want it for yourself.

Money richness can be had in various ways, such as working hard and saving hard. It can also come for free, through an inheritance or win.

A rich life. however, can neither be hard worked nor free. A rich life cannot be haphazard; it must be thought about, through the heart as much as the intellect. It cannot be rushed, nor can it be forced. If you want a rich life then you must align yourself with Life itself, for it is She who dictates which cycle of your life requires more practice, more honing and polishing, and which is ready to be showcased. It is She who shall provide the how, when you are ready, when you are willing. If you are willing to step in line and walk alongside Life, not ahead of Her and nor behind Her, then congratulations! You have chosen the road to a rich life.

Time Cycles – Showing the Way

If we were to observe our responses to Life, we'd find that we operate mostly in a back-to-front, reactive mode. We use up more of our precious time complaining about what we don't like and how difficult people can be, than on strategising a better than average response. We spend more time on what is out of our control, on what happens *to* us, than what is in our control, *our response* to what happens to us. It's possible that you're not aware of doing this. Most people operate on autopilot. If we are realistic, and we need to be, we'll accept that we cannot continue on this path and expect to live a rich life. Changes need to be made, an important one being to allow yourself space. When someone or something pushes those buttons, resist the impulse to react. Give yourself a little head space, a little heart space. As human beings we feel the pain, humiliation and failure as much as the joy, reward and success. It helps to treat yourself kindly. Give yourself time for the dust to settle and then proceed to ask yourself what Life is asking from you, in view of what you've just experienced. From this point you can begin to assume control over yourself and your life.

Time Cycles bring certain experiences which encourage, nudge or push us to respond from our very best qualities. At no time does Life set out to hassle us, to cause us pain or loss. Every experience is intended to motivate you to respond from the very best of who you were born to be. Every experience is intended to be a practice run for you to polish up those very qualities reflected in the number governing your active Personal Time Cycle. Its intention is always to bring out your best through your responses to the experiences it delivers to you. When we don't understand what's going on or the 'why' of it, the challenge and disappointment can knock us off our feet. When we can see the reason behind the experience, when we can see the meaning behind it, then we are back in a position of power – over ourselves and our responses. Eminent psychiatrist, the late Viktor Frankl, endured unspeakable horrors at the hands of the Nazis. In the midst of it all, as he observed himself and his fellow prisoners, he came to the life-sustaining realisation that if we can find meaning in our suffering, in what we don't want, then we can get through almost anything. And in so doing, we evolve and grow into more conscious and more empowered human beings.

This is what I have come to know through Time Cycles – the meaning behind the experience. Throughout my many years of study and in vivo research, with much testing and proving, I have come to know Time Cycles as Universal Laws which exist for the purpose of helping us live a rich and meaningful life. They operate whether we believe in them or not. Whether we work *with* them or unknowingly against them makes no difference to them, but can make a big difference to us – the difference between a mediocre life and a rich and meaningful life. Time Cycles will continue to provide the experiences according to each cycle duration and the numbers which direct them, whether we welcome or resist them. The sun will rise tomorrow whether you believe it will or not. Will you take advantage of the sunshine and get your washing dry? Catch some on your skin perhaps, and increase your vitamin D? Maybe you'll store some as electricity via your solar panels? Alternatively, you can choose to disregard any benefit the sun offers you. Time Cycles operate similarly. Will you choose to use them, to work with them to better your life, or will you disregard them and dismiss any opportunities on offer?

There are overlapping and integrated Universal Time Cycles which direct our world and our personal lives, but the ones I will focus on for the purpose of this book are Personal Time Cycles, or PTC for short. Since I have come to know these allotments of time more closely, I have worked with them. At times when I questioned their validity, I was proven wrong, not they. I believe that when we understand what Life is asking of us, what She expects from us, what She offers us and challenges us with, as reflected within these Time Cycles, and if we are prepared to align ourselves with them, then we can live a rich and meaningful life, regardless of our station. If you are prepared to step up to Life and say 'yes', Life will back you.

When we choose to say yes to the opportunities and we are prepared to meet the challenges reflected in Time Cycles, then we can say with confidence that we are the masters of our lives. Not in a magical or hocus pocus way that delivers to us all that we want, like make-believe, but in a fearless and truthful way, in a realistic and loving way – an authentically powerful way. A way that allows us to respond to our experiences with a quiet confidence. A confidence which inspires us and provides the tools for us to create a life of love, peace and joy, which in turn forms the basis for success and happiness, for good health and wellbeing. This is what it means to live a rich life.

Through Time Cycles we can come to know why certain things happen, or have the potential to happen. When on 8 November 2016, Hillary Clinton went for the top job, the US Presidency, she was in an ending cycle. All sorts of reasons have been given as to why she didn't win the election, but the bottom line is that Life deemed it was not for her at that time. And this was reflected both in her year and day cycles. The US 2016 election provided an excellent piece of research for me. I am a sceptic, and so will only present what I know to be true. If I haven't convinced myself through study, in vivo research or personal experience, I cannot tell you it's true. Donald Trump's Life Profile (LP) chart (more about Life Profiles in my next book) showed a new beginning in the name experience area of his chart. In addition, his Time Cycle for election day also showed a beginning time. Everything in his LP chart showed the presidency was for him, not for Clinton. I shared this with a student of mine, Josephine Biega, when we discussed this over lunch just after the election date had been determined. But – the closest I could bring myself to publicly voicing it, out loud or in the written word, was this statement in an article I wrote for my website, 'He could have waltzed in! Life is offering him leadership on a silver platter. His numbers have been well stacked for this at this time …' (Article, 'US Election', 9 October 2016, AnnaBelcastro.com)

Why could I not voice it? Why could I not say, 'He *will* waltz in', as I knew he would? Because in doing this piece of research, I was hoping beyond hope that because he had run such a brutally negative campaign, Life would *deny* him what She had offered him at that time – leadership. What I learned from this, and for which I am so grateful to both Trump and Clinton, is that what Life offers us is given freely, without strings. Life did not deny Trump the US presidency because he ran a grossly negative campaign, nor because he lacked the political experience, the qualities and skill of diplomacy and protocol which world leaders need. But here's the flipside to this Truth. The choice to accept the presidency was his. Once he said 'yes' to it, the outcome – how he would serve that position, how he would lead his people, how he would relate on the world political stage – was his responsibility. It was for him to wear his leadership along with the impact it would have on the USA and indeed the world. Life would hold him accountable – for his positives and negatives.

Had Clinton and Trump been privy to the information contained in Time Cycles, perhaps Clinton would not have run that year but chosen to wait for 'her time', and perhaps Trump would have surrounded himself with the sharpest intellects he could find so he would be the kind of leader the world needs now. Had he known about and understood Time Cycles, perhaps he would have acknowledged the qualities, abilities and skills he didn't have and sought them in those who did, through his ministry and advisors. But neither were privy to the wisdom contained in Time Cycles and so they missed out on the enormous opportunities available to them to better the lives not only of Americans but the world.

As you can see, this is the kind of inside information that can make the difference between success and failure, happiness and unhappiness, war and peace. And well worth our consideration and application.

Life progresses in cycles of time, which are determined by the number that directs each cycle within that specific span of time. Know this: what Life offers you is there for the taking – it's yours. When you align yourself with what Life offers and work alongside Her, stress loses its intensity, minimising any fallout and maximising success and happiness.

The quiet and sustained confidence it offers, should you decide to integrate and use it in your life, is priceless.

Time Cycles and a Rich Life

Each year of a Major Time Cycle (MTC) comes with a mandate to fulfil. When you come to know and understand what that mandate is, you can choose to work with it or resist it. What you cannot do is to alter that cycle's mandate. Its mission for accomplishment within its span of time comes under Divine jurisdiction. But the choice to meet it or sidestep it, however, is in your jurisdiction, in your control. Up until now, perhaps you were, like most people, unaware of Universal and Personal Time Cycles and their influence in our lives. Perhaps you did not know that walking and working alongside them would open you up to what is needed for growth, maturity and a rich life. When you understand what Life is asking of you, what Divinity is expecting from you, then you have the power to choose, with eyes wide open.

Without this understanding it can seem that everyday life operates on a hit or miss momentum, on the whim of the gods – throwing good fortune in the path of some and denying it to others, exacerbating any stresses or fears. No wonder it's the few rather than the many who believe they have the potential for a rich life. For those who do not share that belief, life can resemble a battleground, a struggle even for survival itself. I'm sure we've all experienced feeling like this at some point in time, even if we haven't vocalised it. But when it becomes a daily occurrence, it can be devastating, debilitating.

Expressions such as, 'It's so hard, I don't know if I can keep going like this', or 'sometimes I don't know what I'm supposed to do', reflect a degree of anguish, a sense of powerlessness that further intensifies the struggle and hopelessness. When we hit a low point in our lives and feel paralysed by our inability to respond, it can leave a sense of loss and sadness in us. When Jack (not his real name) came to see me for a consultation, his business had just folded. Understandably, his self-confidence had also taken a dive. Add to this that he was down to his last few dollars, and it paints a clear picture of why this young man was bordering depression. He told me he was an expert in his field, he knew his job well. In addition, he had planned his finances carefully. When I looked at his Life Profile chart I saw that when he started his business he was in a cycle which offered spiritual expansion, not material expansion. It was not a cycle for starting or going after things but one for going with the flow of things. Any venture begun in such a cycle brings a degree of loss. But of course, Jack knew nothing of Time Cycles, and so blamed himself.

I explained to him the reason why his business had faltered and that it wasn't because he was not good enough, just that his timing was out. Understanding why things happen is often the difference between mustering the courage to give it another go, or retreating to our corner hoping we can stay there forever.

When in 2005 I was diagnosed with advanced breast and lymphatic cancer, I was in a beginning cycle. It took several weeks for me to even consider a therapy plan. Understandably, I was in shock, unable to think clearly, so I gave myself a little time – I needed it. After several weeks my children, fearful that I might opt to not have treatment, became very concerned, but that bit of space allowed me to consider my options carefully before making what would be a life-altering decision.

As a user of complementary medicine, I was not sure which way to go. Would I forgo the post-operative treatment plan my medical team had told me I needed, and opt for more alternative treatment? It was a tough one. My Personal Year Cycle (PYC) called for a response requiring courage and assertiveness. It was a cycle in which any problems were best resolved using the intellect rather than emotions or feelings. In addition, I needed to maintain authority over my life. It was not a time for pulling back and simply going along with what everybody told me I needed to do. This was not scripted into my PYC. It was up to me to decide on a response that ensured the best possible shot for my survival. My life was on the line, literally!

After much thinking and questioning with traditional medical and complementary medical professionals, I decided that due to the cancer having begun to travel through my lymph nodes, taking chances was not something I wanted to entertain. I wanted all the help I could get. I decided to say 'yes' to my medical team and also 'yes' to my naturopath. When I informed my oncologist about my plan to include complementary medicine, he told me I didn't need it. I stood my ground and told him that I wanted it because I knew it would help me. I think he realised that I would have gone with it with or without his consent, so he did not fight me, which I appreciated. He said, 'OK, go ahead, it won't affect what I'm doing.'

I worked with my two therapy teams and I made every change in my life that I believed would help me. I did not hand myself over. I did not relinquish my authority over myself, nor over my therapy. Was it tough? You bet! But I remained in charge of my life within the context of the treatment plan. I aligned myself with the requirements reflected in my PYC and to the best of my ability met all that it asked of me. After six months of heavy-duty chemotherapy, 30 straight daily shots of radiation and a broken arm in between, I sometimes wonder how I got through that annus horribilis. Then at other times I wonder if I truly went through it or was it a figment of my imagination. One thing I'm certain is not a figment of my imagination – my gratitude to everyone involved in my recovery. I am so happy to still be on the planet!

Time Cycles are Life's way of guiding us along the journey to a rich and fulfilling life – a life worth living. They look ahead and warn us of any pebbles or boulders that may call for a redirection or a pit stop. They also tell us when it's time for hard work, when to look at our lives realistically or optimistically, when to push ahead or when to step to the side. They operate for our benefit. Yet, even so, Life, Divinity, The Universe, God, or any other name you have for this loved-up Universal Intelligence, leaves the choice to say yes or no up to us. Undeniably, the ball keeps making its way back in your court.

The Nature of Time Cycles

The Major Time Cycles (MTC) of your birth operate in sequences of nine years. Each of these years I shall refer to as your Personal Year Cycle or PYC for short. After nine years, another MTC begins anew and then another – creating cycles which begin at birth and continue for the remainder of your life. Within the PYCs are shorter Time Cycles which last a month and which are also included in the contents of this book.

Each Personal Year Cycle contains and reflects different qualities and opportunities for growth and advancement – spiritually and materially. Every year Life brings experiences for you to practise the very qualities contained therein. I like to think of each year as a mini degree in the University of Life – offering a major in A Rich Life. The choice to learn and take with you what each PYC offers is of course up to you. But why would you struggle when you can thrive? Why remain in the dark, in the unknowing when you can be in the light, where you can see the unfolding of your life with much more clarity and choice?

Some PYCs focus their attention on the practical and physical aspects of living – the everyday playing field. Others focus on the intellectual areas of reason and logic – the thinking plane. Others emphasise the emotional areas – matters of the heart – while still others focus on the higher plane of Spirit and intuition. Most cycles contain and reflect the human element and its way of relating, of living in the real world, while others are more mystical, bordering on the Divine. Each PYC provides experiences and opportunities towards wholeness; bringing together all the necessary qualities that make us whole – the physical, intellectual, emotional and spiritual.

We can look back at past PYCs and see how much we have grown, how much we have progressed or regressed. This constant nine-year repetition gives us the chance to skill up on certain talents and to take the opportunities presented to us year in, year out. Life's intention is that each time we repeat a cycle of time, we have yet another chance to minimise our negative responses and maximise our positive ones. As you can begin to see, this is intended to encourage steady growth – spiritual and material, gathering momentum towards a rich and meaningful life. Whether at age thirty or seventy, nobody welcomes growing older per se, but I would like to believe that at any age we welcome growing in wisdom and a rich and fulfilling life.

It's All About Timing

Life is difficult, there's no denying it. Motivational speaker of the mid-20th century, Dr Vincent Peale, once said there is only one place one can move to and not have the worries or challenges of everyday living – the local cemetery!

Yes, life is difficult, but it can also be rich and meaningful. We have made life much more difficult than it was meant to be. I was intrigued during a recent TV documentary, as I listened to a young man's lament. He had recently completed a university degree and was having trouble landing a job in his field. At the same time, he refused to consider any other work. He felt that with his professional qualifications he should have the job he trained for and the government should support him until he found that job. When we refuse to see life as it is, when we insist on having what we cannot yet have, we inevitably set ourselves up for failure and a very difficult and miserable life. When we accept that it's normal to experience life's good, bad and in between, we don't feel like victims. We can voice our dislike, we are human after all, but we must accept both what we like and do not like as part and parcel of life.

The number one criterion for a rich and meaningful life is to accept what is, where you are, and be willing to work with that, to give of your best while what you want is still in the field of becoming. Note I said *want,* not *wish.* Wanting something requires effort. If you want something but refuse to put in any effort, then it's a wish. And wishes are the stuff of fairytales – pure fantasy to be enjoyed sparingly, with the knowledge that they are not real.

The biggest favour you can do for yourself is to get real with your lot, now, today. Until you do this, nothing will change for the better and a rich life will remain distant. Consider cooking a meal. The first step is to know what ingredients you have or need to buy. Unless you have magical powers like Samantha, from *Bewitched,* you cannot possibly cook a meal without first getting real, with knowing what ingredients are available to you. Only then can you decide on what you can actually cook. And so it is with a rich and meaningful life.

Each year of your PYC must first be acknowledged and then accepted for its challenges and opportunities and responded to accordingly. We build our lives with our every response to the experiences that come to us through the various cycles of time which govern them. In the words of Buddha, 'If you want to know the past, look at your present. If you want to know the future, look at your present.' We have arrived at where we are today because of our past responses to Life, knowingly or unknowingly. It's for this reason that our response to a situation, to an experience, whether we deem it difficult or easy, just or unjust, is far more important than the situation or experience itself. If you want a rich and meaningful life, then ask yourself if your responses have this purpose in mind. Step outside of yourself. Get out of your own way and look at your responses with eyes wide open. Awareness is what it means to be awake – awake to what Life brings and to the way we process and respond to it.

To be aware is to be able to see clearly. To do this, requires a shift in our thinking, as in our modus operandi. We must switch from auto drive, to manual drive. Making this change is a beginning, and tells us we're serious about what we want. That we're serious about wanting success and happiness, love, peace and joy. The next step is to commit to the maintenance required. If you've ever been on a weight loss diet, you may remember that while the enthusiasm and excitement got the pounds off, keeping them off was another story. Life is similar. Unless you are prepared to keep to manual drive and be constantly aware of your responses, a rich life will keep eluding you. Sure, we all slip into auto drive at times, but the difference is that we know we have done so and we then switch back to manual ASAP. It's like cheating on a diet with one biscuit. It's no big deal, as long as we are aware and then get back on track. Awareness is what it means to come alive. To be alive.

A rich and meaningful life also requires discipline – and discipline comes more easily to some than others. We need discipline to always respond from our very best. This is paramount. If you don't give of your best, you won't get the best. This is your life – ask yourself if you deserve the best possible. If we don't think we deserve that, or if we don't know that it's available to us, or if we are not willing to play our part, it won't happen.

Once we have established that we want a rich and meaningful life, the next step is to follow its timing. Nothing happens before its time. If, for example, you apply for a job for which you are qualified and don't get it, you can give yourself all manner of explanations as to why. Looking at the outcome from a more realistic and higher awareness perspective however, will tell you the reason you didn't get the job was either (a) because Life deemed it wasn't for you, or (b) Life deemed you weren't ready to handle it, yet, in other words it's not the right time for you. When we align ourselves with Life and come to understand, through Times Cycles, our best response, the fear and stress diminishes and the success and happiness maximises.

In early 2016 Sydney house prices had peaked. I had planned to sell my family home of over forty years, but I wasn't ready. I was being told that if I didn't sell very soon, I would miss the market, prices would tumble. But I was not ready. To sell then would have meant that I'd be selling from fear of losing, and I know not to respond out of fear. A decision based on fear does not bring the best possible outcome. It was time to walk my talk, and my future financial security was at stake! I was then in a Three PYC, a time of optimism. I started to prepare the property for sale and gave myself until the end of 2016 to have it ready. The sale price I had originally told myself I'd be happy to receive increased considerably. It matched my overly zealous optimism. A Three cycle can do that. 2016 came and went, and my house was still not up for sale.

It was a May auction in 2017. The market had halted its ascent early that year and the media was feeding uncertainty. I was now in a Four PYC. Not a time to be optimistic, but a time for realism – a time to see things as they were, regardless of my feelings or my financial situation. I knew I had spent money on the house that could have been avoided, but I'm not one for taking shortcuts, I wanted to present it at its best. When bidding stalled at less than my optimistic sale price, I knew my Four PYC demanded a realistic response from me. I accepted the offer and sold. And as my son pointed out to me later that day, the sale price was precisely what I had originally wanted. Had I persisted with the optimism of my previous PYC, I would have lost out, because a month later the market began to dive.

Life delivers accordingly when we step up and align ourselves with Her. If we forge ahead without considering our PYC, its mandate and mission, we can be slowed right down. We can even come to a grinding halt! Saying yes to Life and going *with* the requirements of our current and operative PYC puts us on track to a rich and meaningful life, to success and happiness.

With every ensuing year of your Personal Major Time Cycle, you have the freedom to say yes or no to all that Life offers, asks and expects from you. Whether you say yes or no, the asking and demanding will not cease until that cycle is completed. Life's intention is not to hassle but to teach, to train, to hone and polish, to give you practice runs in certain qualities and specific attributes, always towards wholeness, towards more conscious awareness, towards authentic power. Constantly urging you and at times pushing you, to respond from your best, as you journey towards a rich and meaningful life.

Calculating Your Current Personal Year Cycle

I must stress the importance of working out your Personal Year Cycle correctly. To ensure this, read the method, the 'how to' below, and work out your PYC several times. A miscalculation will understandably give you inaccurate information. As you can appreciate, accuracy in your calculations is a must.

Please note - You will also find calculations for your PYC on my website AnnaBelcastro.com. Go to *Weekly Numbers or Numbers for the Month*.

You may prefer to use pen and paper for your calculations. Your year of birth is not required, only your day and month of birth. To work out your Personal Year Cycle, add together the numbers of the day and month of your birth to the numbers of the year you last celebrated your birthday. This will be either the current calendar year, or the previous year.

At the time of this book's publication the calendar year was 2019, so the examples below are calculated with this in mind. For the purpose of this exercise and to maintain simplicity you can *add* the day, month and year straight across. Here are two examples:

Example 1:

For someone born 31 December.
Write down the day and year of your birth along with the calendar year you last celebrated your birthday in numeric form:
31 - 12 - 2018
Now add the numbers together:
$3 + 1 + 1 + 2 + 2 + 0 + 1 + 8 = 18$

Now add these two numbers together: 1 + 8 = **9**
Your current Personal Year Cycle (PYC) is **9**
Always reduce the numbers to a final single digit.

Example 2:

For someone born 20 January.
Write down the day and year of your birth along with the calendar year you last celebrated your birthday in numeric form:
20 - 1 - 2019
Now add the numbers together:
2 + 0 + 1 + 2 + 0 + 1 + 9 = 15
Now add these two numbers together: 1 + 5 = 6
Your current Personal Year Cycle (PYC) is **6**

Though the Calendar Year Cycle runs from January to December, your Personal Year Cycle runs from birthday to birthday and changes with every birthday.

When Do I Calculate my Personal Year Cycle?

You won't need to calculate your PYC every birthday. Each PYC runs in sequence. If you are currently in a Six PYC, with your next birthday you will move into a Seven PYC. If you are currently in a Nine PYC, with your next birthday you will move into a One PYC, and so on.

Understand that Numbers and Time Cycles themselves do not make things happen, they merely interpret what is encoded and reflected therein. The invitation to the opportunities offered is extended – however, the decision to say yes or no to its requirements is up to you. How closely you choose to align yourself to the requirements needed and specified within each Time Cycle to enable you to take its opportunities will establish the degree of success and happiness attainable.

Though the experience is there to be taken, the ultimate outcome is always dependent on the choices you make. Nothing surpasses free will. Whatever the experience, how you choose to respond to it, is up to you. The choice is yours. Most of the experiences that come to us are everyday ones. You might even think them of no great importance. And while you may consider them not life changing, they can be. Because with every response you make, you set up another scene of your life within the context of what's scripted in your Life Profile (more about this in my next book) and your PYC.

Consider this scenario. Say, for example, I invite you to have lunch with me. You have no control over that. It's something that has come to you. Life has brought that to you. Your response however, is very much in your control and will determine the next scene of your life with me, within the context of that invitation. What is your choice? You can choose to say no, and by so doing, stop that opportunity from eventuating. Our lunch scene is halted in the field of possibility. It does not move into the reality field. It does not happen. You can choose to say yes, and with that 'yes' Life proceeds to set up the lunch scene and move it into the reality field. That very lunch scene in your life with me then moves from possibility stage to becoming stage, along with new opportunities. As you can see, your every response carries potential. This example allows a glimpse into just how powerful and life changing your choices can be. Life, God, Universal Intelligence, call It what you will, constantly brings you experiences, some small, some grand, to prompt and encourage you to always choose what carries the capacity for a rich and meaningful life – but leaves the choice up to you. For your part, it's important to know that that choice will determine the outcome. And with every choice, with your every response, you create your life. This is what it means to be co-creators with God.

Now you are ready to read your Personal Year Cycle!

Part 2:

Personal Year Cycles

All human life has its seasons and cycles, and no one's personal chaos can be permanent. Winter, after all, gives way to spring and summer, though sometimes when branches stay dark and the earth cracks with ice, one thinks they will never come that spring and that summer, but they do, always.

– TRUMAN CAPOTE

One
Personal Year Cycle

The ONE Personal Year Cycle brings experiences intended to hone and polish the following qualities and areas of life –

Leadership, Creative Thinking, Problem Solving, Individuality, Invention, Determination, Courage, Foresight, Innovation, Executive Ability, Individuation, Strength of Purpose.

Its mandate is to prompt, encourage and at times push you to live these qualities to the very best of your ability in positive mode, and in so doing promote and sustain a constant state of evolving and becoming the whole and truly unique person you were born to be.

The ONE Personal Year Cycle

In life everything is punctuated with a beginning and an end. This is your beginning time. Think of it as Life offering you a fresh start. Using your wisdom and planning on an intellectual level will set the tempo for this year. Expect lots of activity as a new nine-year cycle of experience gets underway. Take the initiative and set the goals for what you want to accomplish. Look at this year as a launching pad for the next nine years of your life and as a marked pit stop to the rest of your life.

This is the best time to make plans for the future, so do your homework and carefully consider any advice given to you. Then have the courage and confidence to follow through with your decisions. This is not a time to limit your ideas, aim for the moon or the sun – and as they say, even if you don't reach that far, it makes catching a star or two a real possibility. Focus on plans for the future, on where you want to be and do. Details are not necessary now, but knowing what you want is. It doesn't mean everything you plan will happen, or that it will happen this year. Avoid getting hung up on that. Remember, plans are as much about the future as the present. This is not the cycle for deciphering your dreams or culling this one or that one.

Thinking of starting a new business, a new job or perhaps a new relationship? Then make your choices, for it's a beginning time on all fronts. What you do this year will have an effect on the next nine years of your life, so please pay attention to your thoughts and actions. This cycle is such that it demands you put your best foot forward and have the courage to make your own decisions. Not haphazardly, but with much reasoning and intellectual logistics. Whatever Life delivers to your door, face it. Facing an issue is the first step towards resolving it. In whatever form it takes – a lottery win, an illness, a changed relationship, a new home, or anything else that lands on your doorstep. That's what courage is. You must take charge; you must call the shots and respond with a quiet confidence. This doesn't mean you cannot accept help, but it does mean that you do not take a back seat and hand yourself over to someone or something.

This year the buck stops with you, so delegate more if it's necessary, it's what leaders do. Don't worry if it doesn't all happen now, but do make plans for tomorrow's destinations, ideas, goals, plans and start-ups. You will feel a surge of energy as you sense an ambition and drive for betterment, even if you cannot name the 'what for' of it. Take the opportunity life is now offering you. If you are not out to change much, do something that will expand your mind and give you a fresh perspective on things, on the old, on what's already established, mentally or in reality. Life is pushing you to stand on your own two feet, towards independence, leadership and self-reliance. Sure, it's not a walk in the park. This year you will have to depend more on yourself than on others if you wish to accomplish.

Take care of your health, especially in the early part of the calendar year. Mental interests and mental creativity are a part of this cycle's mandate. Put your mental attributes to work this year. Think more and don't be afraid to ask the necessary questions. Expect change, something new, or renewed. Consider you may be facing a turning point in your life. Just take a while to sit with that, with the importance of this reality. You cannot change the past, so let go of what is unwanted if you have not already done so. Trim or cut the strings to anything or anyone not for you – not for your spiritual growth, wellbeing and success.

Do not be surprised if something you planned to finish up last year, reaches its conclusion this year. Let go of all the stuff you do not wish to take with you into this new beginning cycle. Your future is in your hands. When you respond to the new opportunities in this cycle's mandate, and use these for the benefit of others as well as yourself, success can be yours.

Your best responses during a One Personal Year Cycle
- Assume control of your life.
- Be confident in your abilities without being pompous.
- Use your foresight to see where your plans can take you.
- Let go of anything that denies your spiritual mandate.
- Plan for what you want to achieve, state your goals, write them down. Own them.
- Know what you want, be deliberate. Life does not require you to know 'the how', but it does require you to know 'the what'.
- Make use of this beginning time, wherever you find yourself.
- Accept that you cannot do it all now, but plan you must, now.
- Look to the future with a quiet and courageous confidence.

January in a ONE Personal Year Cycle

If you are planning to spend January on your lonesome, don't bank on it. It's not that kind of month. It's more about inviting or allowing others into your life, not pushing them out. At the same time though, be gracious in giving them the space they may need. Keep an open mind and make time for quiet and tranquillity, even in the busyness of what is going on around you. It's in this way you will open yourself up to receiving the help you may need or want. Anticipation of change connected to improvements in home and business may be on your mind, but avoid feeling uneasy when something does not go according to plan. Take the opportunity to make any necessary adjustments. Look at the little things that are often missed because we haphazardly deem them unimportant. Yet, these can often make the difference.

Though there is much to do, you might find the sense of urgency and drive lacking, and that's OK. The pace of the month is deliberately slow, but it's still in forward motion. Prepare in any way necessary for what may assist you to keep on track. Be aware of the possibility for a change to what had been planned, as others may not deliver on your expectations. Your peacemaking qualities may be tested as your sensitivity and vulnerability to what is said to you, or how others treat you, is exposed. It's in your best interest to maintain your ideals and stay tuned to that higher level of knowing. Look beyond the ordinary and the mundane. When things don't go according to plan find a quiet spot and allow yourself to be Divinely guided. Give those in your life the benefit of the doubt before passing sentence on them, so to speak. Be diplomatic, be sociable, be adaptable to people and situations, and step away from taking non urgent or unimportant things too seriously.

Your best responses for January
- Be a team player.
- Avoid rushing ahead of Life's plans for you.
- Be sensitive to the needs and faults of others, as well as your own.
- Be more cooperative than assertive.
- You need others this month, so be accommodating and gentle in your responses.

February in a ONE Personal Year Cycle

In a year intent on showcasing your leadership and assertiveness potential, February encourages you to include something more. Self-expression through artistic and creative interests is on the cards. Now is the time for you to take part in that workshop or course you've been thinking about. Be sure to include any genre that stimulates intellectual creativity. What's the movie playing in your mind? If you see yourself kicking up your heels, then go ahead – be as a kid again, even if it's only make believe. You need to be optimistic now. If you want friends in your life, then you will need to be a friend. Pick up the phone and organise a leisurely lunch with the special others in your life. At the same time, be sure to resist any inclination to spend more than your wallet or credit card comfortably allows. Emotions will be stirred, so do your best to keep them within positive range. Coerce your courage into making an entrance and stand tall to support you.

It's possible that someone with a strong or aggressive attitude may try to dampen your happiness or enthusiasm. If you are confused about certain issues, wait until your head is clear before making any changes. Do not allow indecision to stop you from moving forward. Stand your ground assertively and have the courage to make your own decisions, but only after you gather the facts, and get any advice which may assist you Maintaining control over a situation may prove challenging, as your sensitive side seeks to dominate. Others may not be on the same wavelength, so don't feel wounded if they don't respond with the same sensitivity and enthusiasm as yourself. Sharp or negative reactions will not serve you well and are best avoided – the better option is for a confident and positive response. Purposely immerse yourself in the happiness Life intends for you.

Your best responses for February
- Be optimistic without going overboard and missing what's real.
- Do something to make you happy.
- Connect with others, socially and in friendship.
- Enjoy life more, be more light-hearted.
- Showcase your creative abilities – intellectual, emotional, physical.

March in a ONE Personal Year Cycle

This is a month when all things practical take precedence. Any issues are best resolved from a base of reality spiced with sensitivity. It's a time when being more realistic rather than purely optimistic will win for you. So look at the facts and prepare yourself to meet this month's requirements head on, even if your emotions say otherwise. Family and the domestic scene will also take centre stage. Any health matters, yours or those of loved ones, will need to be attended to. Meet all commitments without feeling overwhelmed. Put your energy into what needs to be done rather than getting flustered and confused. Going at a hundred miles an hour is not recommended and will only slow any progress in the making. But March is not all about hard work, it's not about denying your social life, it's about *deliberately* making time for it.

Watch out for that sensitivity and don't take what others say to heart. Defog your mind and get all the facts, including the 'insignificant' ones, before making any decisions. Do not allow resentment, heaviness or anger to get in the way of what can be achieved. Seeing the situation realistically will help bring about the best possible outcome and a more relaxed environment. Reassure yourself of your capabilities and strength as you take care of what beckons with sound organisation and good management. Sure, your vulnerability cannot be denied, and that's OK, as long as you don't lose yourself in it. This month brings you the opportunity to lay a foundation for something; something, which can pay dividends not only in future months, but also in future years. It all however, rests on your ability to positively mobilise that element of sensitivity and blending it with all things practical. Be sure to make time for, and include spending time with those close to you.

Your best responses for March
- Meet any duties and obligations willingly, with grace and a quiet confidence.
- Make your sensitivity work for you, not against you. Refuse to fall into victimhood.
- Good people skills will win for you.
- Look at your life and see where you stand, what you have, then work with that as your base, towards what you want in the future.
- Avoid rushing – take it slow, take it steady.

April in a ONE Personal Year Cycle

This will be a busy month with lots on your calendar. You will feel a sense of freedom, even if it doesn't come with a card that allows you to change all that you do not like. As you pick up on what's going on around you, you will come to see that some changes are inevitable. At the same time it is also encouraging to note that some things have moved into the progressive lane. The lighter feel will have you wanting to do so much that you may find yourself taking on more than you can give your time to. Feelings of restlessness and uncertainty are best contained as you test the waters with the possibilities of what's to come.

Leave any negative criticism behind you and accept that nobody's perfect, yourself included. Joy and enthusiasm are in your challenge position, so effort will be required in this department. Do your best to maintain focus on the love and joy that is already in your life, rather than focusing on what's not there at this time. Make time for socialising and enjoying the company of friends and loved ones. Changes abound, so consider these wisely before acting on them. Do not be surprised if you spend some time away from home. Being resourceful and flexible will help you make any necessary adjustments when dealing with surprises or something you had not anticipated. Respond without getting hot-headed about it or becoming unrealistic – stay calm and think straight. Avoid overdoing things and causing your health to suffer. Be prepared for the unexpected and enjoy the people connection. Be sure to maintain an optimistic frame of mind and express your feelings instead of keeping them locked up inside you. The way you communicate your wants and needs can take you far – so be focused and be gentle rather than haphazard in your strategies here.

Your best responses for April
- Maintain a positive attitude.
- People interaction brings opportunity.
- Make an effort to understand, rather than criticise.
- Communication is key, make it work for you and not against you.
- Nurture good friendships.

May in a ONE Personal Year Cycle

You cannot hide from the world this month. High expectations give way to caring and prioritising what needs to be done. It's important that you add a degree of organisation and structure to your plans, and avoid rushing anything through. Give careful consideration to what's important, and ask for help if it will lessen your load. Health issues need to be attended to rather than placed on the backburner. There will be lots do as you feel the sense of responsibility for yourself and others weighing on your shoulders. Avoid becoming headstrong – just be strong. Fairness and compromise will make you the winner. This is not the time for self-interest or self-pity as objectivity sets the stage for decision making. Accept the help that others offer and enjoy the love given and expressed – you deserve it! Do not worry unduly about finances now; money will be available to meet your requirements.

Understand that while you have your ideals and live your life accordingly, others may not feel the same way. Think about it; if you have your standards and see fit to engage them in business and personal relationships, then is it not also fair that others will also want to live according to their own standards and ideals? At the same time be aware that others, out of love and concern for you, may try to convince you to see things from their perspective. May is a month of compromise, adjustments, good judgement and rewards. It's not about how things *should* be, but about doing the best you can with what's available to you. Self-care is important now. Family members will have well-meaning intentions so don't come down too hard on them if they try to *do what's best for you.* Enjoy the family socials, the joy and unconditional love that little ones give so generously.

Your best responses for May
- You are the humanitarian this month.
- Celebrate your part as a member of family and community.
- Show someone you care.
- Be gracious in accepting the love, care and support offered you.
- Slow down, take as much time as you need for all worthwhile decisions.

June in a ONE Personal Year Cycle

June is a good time to mark some 'time out' for yourself. If you feel you need to move away from a stressful situation, do so. You may feel uncertain about some aspects of your relationships, which may be linked to current circumstances and where you are in life right now. And that's understandable. If you are feeling restless or critical about what others are doing or not doing, be aware that the intensity of the situation could be a consequence of how you are seeing things right now. Consider indulging in a good strong dose of faith in yourself instead. In a month when your numbers indicate that you are not calling the shots, perhaps trusting in that Higher Power is the better option. It may seem to you that your life is at a standstill when in fact Life is asking you to shift into low gear and walk alongside Her instead of ahead of Her. Time and least resistance is required now. Life is asking you to trust that in the big picture, all is well.

For sure, you may not be as free as a bird, but this is not the time to force things. Even though the feel of the month is more introspective than out there, it is nonetheless paralleled with a great deal of activity. So, maintain confidence and certainty in your ability. Attend to any matters that beckon and make sure others are not attempting to take advantage of you. Your independence may be somewhat thwarted, but do not allow this to bring out your negative side. If you feel down, refuse to take to your corner indefinitely, but rather make more time to do more of what can elevate your moods – taking in a movie, buying something new, reading, meditating, or simply enjoying quiet times with an understanding friend or partner. June is about quality, not quantity.

Your best responses for June
- Accept that it's OK to step to the side occasionally, in idle mode.
- Participate more as an observer.
- Enjoy quality time with the most important person in your life – YOU!
- Be selective with whom you share yourself this month – only those who have the best intentions for you.
- Respond not from emotion but from wisdom.

July in a ONE Personal Year Cycle

It's a great feeling to find that you are now getting on top of things, so indulge yourself – allow yourself to feel that inner sense of security, self-esteem and mind control. Much will be expected from you as Life tests your strength, resilience and endurance. Take control of your life and respond to all that it brings you with benefits in mind. You may feel driven to do more, but avoid going at top speed. Be sure to look at both sides of the situation when a decision is called for. July is the month for you to put those plans into action. Look at situations objectively and use your judgement wisely to assess circumstances as they truly are, rather than as they appear to be. This is the time for you to make your confidence, skills and abilities work for you. Take action and get things done which will benefit your situation. Thoughts or issues connected to property, buying or selling or perhaps renovations around the home or place of work are on the cards, and may take up some of your time. Business ventures needing rearrangement may also surface this month. Money matters may be a little strained, however, you need not go into overdrive about this – ensures that you balance your spending with your available budget and all will come together.

Be responsible in regard to your health and wellbeing. Bring balance into all that you do. It's not about pushing yourself to do more than you can comfortably manage, and do accept the help that's offered to you. Refuse to get frazzled when others get themselves into negative situations that you could see happening a mile away. A business trip could be on the cards. You should feel a sense of satisfaction due to what you have managed this month even if not all you expected materialised.

Your best responses for July
- Show your strength; face what needs to be addressed.
- Take control, without being controlling.
- Include rest and leisure activities as part of the month.
- Take care of your health.
- Delegate more.

August in a ONE Personal Year Cycle

Your feelings and emotions will be at the wheel this month. There is the possibility of something connected to the past reaching a conclusion or finality – in the realm of your mind if not in actuality. Though last year was the year to finalise things, Life is not black and white, hence the possibility of finishing the ending you began processing last year. You cannot have new beginnings without putting to rest what is no longer relevant or sustainable in your life. Doing this will enable you to move forward with the full force of your One PYC with a more positive feeling in regard to where your plans and achievements have brought you so far.

Information may come to you that you may not be happy about – let it go. Approach all that is now in your life, including your own vulnerability, with understanding, empathy and forgiveness. Make your heart big enough to want good things for others as well as for yourself. Life will expect you to be compassionate and understanding and to approach things from an impersonal base. You may feel moments of nostalgia as you contemplate what might have been. Do not allow these feelings to deepen into low moods, merely acknowledge them and allow them to pass. Entertainment is in the air, as also anything connected to the arts. Take in a concert or some other light form of entertainment – do something that makes you happy. Say yes to all your social invitations and allow yourself to truly feel the flow of life – be grateful for the good that has come your way. Choose to respond to everything from that wonderful level of intuitive guidance and know that in the big picture, all is well.

Your best responses for August
- Be prepared to put the 'finished' stamp on something.
- Refuse to linger on what might have been.
- Be willing to forgive past hurts to enable you to move forward minus the baggage.
- Accept that you cannot change the past.
- Feel the wonder and enormity of Universal Oneness and your special place in it.

September in a ONE Personal Year Cycle

You will feel a sense of inspiration and confidence this month, even your energy levels feel at their peak. It's all up to you, so be encouraged and determined that you have what it takes to meet Life's offerings. A One PYC is intended to polish and hone initiative, self-reliance, foresight, intellectual creativity, problem solving and courage. These are the very qualities needed for success and happiness this year. Perhaps by now you have a sense of satisfaction at just how much you have accomplished. Or maybe more time is needed to see results. Take time to rest as the mental strain of the year could take its toll on your health.

Your assertiveness may edge towards its limit during September, when your buttons are pushed in ways you do not like. Respond assertively, not aggressively and you will get much more of what you want and need. Refuse to let your sensitivity stop you from doing the things that bring you pleasure and enjoyment. Such things are good for the soul as well as the heart. For anything challenging, take a step back for a more expansive view of the situation and then consider your options. When Life asks too much from you, delegate more. You may feel overwhelmed, but only if you insist on doing it all on your own. The other option is to say 'no' if it means maintaining a peaceful disposition. Use the leadership and executive skills offered in your One PYC as needed, and make use of everything you have learned so far. Make a conscious decision to prioritise your workload and commitments, this will give you time for the 'play' of life, which is just as essential as the 'work' of life.

Your best responses for September
- Take charge, the ball is in your court.
- Avoid making money a priority over life's necessities.
- Courage will take you to the next base.
- •It's time to look ahead, to where you want to go, to where you want to be.
- Lead and take charge more, manage and labour hard, less.

October in a ONE Personal Year Cycle

There is no real rush imposed upon you this month. You will find that even if you push harder for what you want, it won't happen. The little things that are often missed or considered insignificant make a difference. So, ease up, get the necessary details together and whatever else is essential for what you are planning and know that things are moving along even if not as fast as you'd like. Others will be there to help, perhaps even someone with a degree of clout – be gracious in accepting. Put any sensitivity and timidity aside and ask for what you need instead of waiting in expectation for someone to offer. Someone might come across as knowing what's best for you. If this is the case avoid succumbing to feelings of smallness or frustration. Rather, be self-confident and refuse to be put on the spot for any answers you are unsure about. Resolving problems with tact and understanding will help you when you are asked for a favour that goes beyond your acceptable quota of generosity.

In a One PYC *your* happiness and wellbeing should be at the top of the list, right alongside those you love. Social outings, friends and loved ones will add to the people orientation of the month. Good management and efficiency will ensure that what's got to be done now will not be carried over to next month. October's numbers indicate an all or nothing option. There is the opportunity to truly shine in some way, or you can just plod along and get stuck in neutral gear. The month's offerings are such that you can achieve all that is achievable or if you refuse to budge from neutral gear, achieve little if anything. The choice is yours to make. I encourage you to move out of neutral and go for the 'all'.

Your best responses for October
- Be kind, be grateful, be gracious – in asking and in receiving.
- Make time to notice and appreciate the little things.
- Join with others to make good things happen.
- Add a little honey to the mix.
- Be the host/hostess.

November in a ONE Personal Year Cycle

In a month when Life asks you to showcase your creative talent and positive attitude, She is also asking you to adopt a quiet disposition of sustained confidence. Believe in yourself and have the courage to follow through with what's important to your self-improvement. Use the mental control that your One PYC offers you, and implement as you wish, as you know to be for the best. If you feel that someone is trying to exert a stronger will over you, remind yourself that you are capable of handling this. There's no need for aggressive tactics, nor for retreating inside yourself. It's a steady and assertive attitude that will bring it home for you. For sure, you can sense lots of ideas filtering through at this time in connection to what you foresee yourself doing in future years. Mental and intellectual activity is on a high note. Creative, artistic, exciting, visual, enthusiastic – these are the words to describe what is being reflected and on offer in November's numbers. Indulge in something that makes you happy. You will feel a certain *gioia di vivere* iced with a sensual mood for carefree fun and social stimulation.

Enjoy the inspiration of the month. Spend time with friends, with those who inspire you. Life's intention is for joy – in giving and receiving through a delightful light heartedness. Watch your moods and do not allow them to mar the sincerity in what you share with those in your life. Self-improvement and not self-importance should be on your mind. Consider the difference between the two and you will gain from this. Visualise what you wish to attract into your life and replay it in your mind as an affirmation to ensure ultimate success. If you are Christmas shopping, be aware of the impulse to overspend. Be sure to keep within your budget to avoid any regrets later. Enjoy the admiration and the inspiration!

Your best responses for November
- Be optimistic without being unrealistic.
- Express your feelings with joy, sincerity and decorum.
- Inspire and be inspired.
- Be as a child – in awe of Life's beauty.
- Dream a little. Be enthusiastic.

December in a ONE Personal Year Cycle

While everyone around you appears to be indulging in the festive mood of the Christmas and holiday season, Life asks you to also include and attend to all things practical and necessary. Be happy with where you are in your journey during this One PYC – you have come a long way. At the same time, do not drop your guard just yet. If there are documents or legal papers to take care of, or perhaps business issues to attend to, do so with seriousness and a clear mind. Avoid making a rushed decision on important matters and make certain you are not overlooking something that may be significant, though not standing out. Be economical in your approach and pay any outstanding accounts. Meet your obligations willingly. If you get the feeling that money is not there for the more pleasurable things in life, you're absolutely right. This month does not give you the go ahead to spend on those personal extras, but it's a yes for what is needed, including gifts. It's a busy time with social activities on the cards but be sure to make time for your health. Life asks you to be strong and not wear your heart on your sleeve as you deal with what is, rather than what you would like it to be.

Family features this month and some aspects may feel more heavy than enjoyable. Be aware of your sensitivity here. Remind yourself of all you have achieved so far and of how deep your reserves are. If necessary, compromise to get what you want. Enjoy the festivities with those who hold a little piece of your heart, in your own special way.

Your best responses for December
- Give yourself the special care you would give someone you love.
- Refuse to get stuck in Life's heaviness when others avoid their responsibilities.
- Do not allow yourself to take on too much.
- Be realistic.
- Keep in mind that though you may not have a magic wand, you can do and give of your very best, and in this way your outcomes shall also be the best possible.

Two
Personal Year Cycle

The TWO Personal Year Cycle brings experiences intended to hone and polish the following qualities and areas of life –

Partnerships, Relationships, Tact and Diplomacy, Mediation, Peaceful Negotiation, Gentleness, Information Collection, Cultural Refinement, Spiritual Awareness, Cooperation, Adaptability, Sensitivity.

Its mandate is to prompt, encourage and at times push you to live these qualities to the very best of your ability in positive mode, and in so doing promote and sustain a constant state of evolving and becoming the whole and truly unique person you were born to be.

The TWO Personal Year Cycle

The degree of success and happiness achievable this year will depend on your people skills. This year's cycle, under the direction of the Number Two, is among other things a cycle of relationships and partnerships. Life's intention this year is to hone and polish your skills in relating to others. To know your place in a relationship, in your true capacity – as a romantic partner, as an employee, as a sibling etc. Much of your time will be spent with others, both socially and in business. In addition, what others can do for you is also a part of this year's intent for honing and polishing those very skills. It's about working with others, more so than on your own. It's not a time for you to shy away from asking for help if you need it. Refuse to entertain any negative feelings about this. You may find that at some stage you will need help and support, that some things, for one reason or another, you cannot do for yourself. The better results will come about by liaising and working with others. Coming up with ideas and resolutions through combined effort rather than individual effort alone.

The emotional sensitivity that is so much a part of this Two PYC, may bring some soul-searching experiences. Keep in mind that it is in your best interest to steer away from impulsive responses. Laying blame on others when things do not go as you would like, will not fix things. Neither will shifting into victim mode help you. Pointing the finger accusingly when someone in your life acts in a manner you do not approve will only take you backwards. Of course this does not mean that you dismiss hurt or aggression. Should you decide to end a relationship, then let it be with consideration and without bitterness for all concerned. It's a Time Cycle which rewards the gentler side of human nature – strength and confidence married with kindness, tact and diplomacy. This doesn't mean you have to walk over people, but be more a negotiator and diplomat to get your point across.

Understand that everything is as it should be. Feel comfortable with where you are right now. If you play your cards right, applying less force and more cooperation and persuasion to get what you want, you'll be amazed at the help and support that comes your way. This is a year intended for sharing good times with those special others in your life. It's a year with a focus on relationships – from intimate relationships, to friends, business acquaintances, the cleaner, the boss, siblings, the checkout operator and anyone else who crosses your path. It is a year when friendships and relationships can be made stronger, can be loosened or even cut. If you can see a relationship which you want to maintain loosening, then shift into repair mode and make the changes needed to bring about the result you want. At the same time, understand that some things are out of our control. If that's the case then let it be, let it go – with love and goodwill for the other as well as yourself.

Convince yourself to maintain a positive attitude, and work with rather than in opposition to others. But before you can do this, you will need to collect your evidence. Ask yourself who is for you. Who has good intentions for you and who is using you. Spend more time with the former and less or none at all with the latter. Work with those in your life in a more coherent way, whether for personal needs or in the world of business. Using negotiation and compromise in your relationships will see you come out on top. Be prepared as your peacemaking qualities will be tested. Someone or some situation will push you to react. This is Life's way of bringing you experiences and opportunities to encourage you to choose a response which showcases your best. And this year your best is as a promoter of peace and harmony. It's understandable that we can love someone deeply, yet also know that to live with them would mean to deny ourselves peace and joy.

Excitement, new contacts, surprises, enjoyment and social interaction are on this year's calendar. Time is needed, so avoid rushing or getting ahead of yourself. Consider your ideas and your future goals. Take off your roller skates and move into cruise control. This is not a time for impatience or intolerance. Understand that what Life is offering you and your own plans, what you want to achieve, will take time to reach maturity. And that's OK.

Approach any issues that may arise with the intention of bringing beneficial results for the other person as well as yourself, and you will find that by year's end problems will be resolved.

Your best responses during a TWO Personal Year Cycle
- Be more cooperative than pushy.
- Say 'yes' more often to social invitations.
- Offer a compromise rather than a 'win at any cost'.
- Be gentle, be kind, be gracious, but do not be a pushover.
- Include others in your life.
- Consider the little things, for they will underpin the big things.
- Know who is for you and who is there for what they can get from you.
- Be sensitive to others' needs as well as your own.
- Make sure your responses are justified and not defensive.
- Build bridges for the future, strengthen good connections.

January in a TWO Personal Year Cycle

This month Life gives you permission to put yourself first. Self expression is encouraged and self interest can be entertained throughout January. Remember though that self expression does not mean self righteousness. Have you been ignoring that creative talent of yours? Has it been lying dormant within you? Now's a good time to brush away the cobwebs and allow it expression. Consider ways you would enjoy and promote self improvement, self expression and artistic pursuits in your life. These are on the agenda for January, in your mind if not in actuality. You may choose to pursue a new interest such as writing, dance, cooking, exercise, floral art, public speaking, sketching or any other activity that interests you. Keep in mind that creativity can be as much about expression through the mind and intellect as through the emotional and physical sense. You will feel an interest in utilising that creative impulse this month. Don't dismiss it, give it a go. Perhaps you can invite a friend to join you.

It may be difficult to be as organised or as in control as you'd like, so be adaptable to the surprise element which may surface. Be aware, as emotions rule this month, as does communication. For your part you need to make sure both are expressed with sincerity as well as fun and joy. Make them work for you, not against you. This month's experiences may include some bittersweet moments. Accept these feelings without allowing them to develop into low moods. Your emotions may be touched for sadness as well as for joy. Social activities and friendships add enjoyment and offer possibility for the unexpected. Share your interests with friends as there will be much to talk about. You will sense the admiration that others have for you and get a buzz from this. There is a touch of romance in the air! Step back and observe – consider what you can do to step up areas that will enhance your personality and your character. Friends and social activities add enjoyment to the light-hearted feel intended for January. Do something for yourself no other reason than the joy it stirs in you.

Your best responses for January
- Be sociable without being extravagant.
- Be aware – friendships can be loosened or strengthened.
- Avoid gossip, make your responses reflect your best qualities.
- Be optimistic without being unrealistic.
- Envision the possibilities

February in a TWO Personal Year Cycle

The practical aspect of this month asks that you deal with any issues, even those caused by others, with clarity of mind. Much of your time spent on the economical and practical issues of life may well be connected to the dealings of those in your life at this time. It's important that you give whatever time may be necessary to resolving matters so that these are not carried over into March. Doing what needs to be done now will mean more free time next month. If you're feeling more stubborn than cooperative, then be sure to keep it in check, especially if it threatens to undo the good work already in progress. Be willing to listen to what others have to say with an open mind, even if your initial reaction is to say 'no'. There may be something in what is being offered or suggested that could benefit you. It's a month when obligations and promises are best met with sympathy and kindness. In addition, handling any relationship issues, business or personal, with understanding and diplomacy, will ensure the better outcome. Attend to all documents with efficiency, especially if it's your signature required on the dotted line.

There is much on your 'to do' list during February, but that doesn't mean you have to neglect your health and wellbeing. Consult medical help if you need to. If you feel somewhat restricted this month, not being totally free to be and do as you would like, you're not mistaken.

Feelings of frustration may also enter in, especially when things appear to move at a slower pace than you would like. Much can be gained when you convince yourself to work with what you have rather than what you don't have. Concentrate on your plans or you may find next to nothing has been achieved at month's end. Others may expect much from you, so do share the load. Make time for and enjoy social outings with family and friends amidst the practical requirements of the month.

Your best responses for February
- Make plans, be organised and methodical.
- Be prepared to work – and then delight in your accomplishments.
- Take whatever time is needed, don't rush.
- Be more practical than sensitive.
- Be supportive without carrying the load.

March in a TWO Personal Year Cycle

It's always a good feeling when we are moving forward in life instead of backwards. Allow yourself to feel the exhilaration as this month's energy begins to make itself felt. Expect changes, perhaps even to the plans of the previous month, and possibly due as much to the involvement of others. Life's intention for the month is for growth and improvement through change. Change that come to you and changes you yourself make. Do ponder the opportunities Life offers you, and also those you yourself have glimpsed, but always with the consideration of others in mind. It is not wise to cast others aside in the foolish notion that you no longer need them. This is not about burning any bridges, but about maintaining access to and travelling on those you have already built. Keep any impulsiveness in check as you choose your words carefully to ensure they deliver the results you want. Stand up for what you believe in with confidence and minus any personal criticism.

Maintaining a handle on things may prove challenging, so make a conscious effort to do so by assuming control over your responses. Attend to legalities wisely as there is an element of surprise running through the month. Avoid overdoing as this could strain your health. Make time for leisure – it's good for the soul as well as the body. Travel is on the cards, within your own shores, abroad or simply moving around more in your local area. Join in to support community and social committees; this can also offer a chance to expand your own circle. March is a people month, not a time for you to hide from the world. Should you become restless, do something – rearrange the furniture or buy something new for yourself, as your bank balance allows, of course. Enjoy the activity and social interaction of the month.

Your best responses for March
- Be flexible, be like a willow.
- Be sure to know and understand the rules if your intention is to bend them.
- Understand, though, that breaking them is a definite 'no go zone'.
- Consider the opportunities on offer and then consider your options.
- Make sure any changes you make will better your life.

April in a TWO Personal Year Cycle

The domestic scene features this month and responsibilities connected to both family and work related matters will be there for you. The care element wrapped up in what Life asks of you translates into supporting and lending a hand as the need arises. It's what you do for others that determines your degree of success and happiness during April. This month you are called to serve. Not as a servant, but as one who is willing to help, utilising your skills and talents. A time which encourages you to showcase your good character and standing. Don't be surprised if business associates expect you to take more on board. Be prepared for family members who will want a little piece of you. This may include caring for someone needing help in a medical way. Then again that 'someone' could be you. At times you may feel that you do so much and nobody appreciates any of it. Do not allow these feelings to develop into resentment, as stress could result in illness. Remember that love must accompany every action if it is to come back to you in the way you expect. Those on the receiving end will notice the intent behind what you do this month.

You can become overly sensitive to the directions others give you, or the assumptions they make. It's understandable that your sensitivity may surface, but more importantly refrain from taking what they say as a direct reflection of your character. Attend to all commitments such as legalities, paying bills or repairing things as they come up, rather than putting them aside for later. You may feel the desire to beautify your surroundings, to spend a little on what you love and those you love, and that's OK. Love is in the air and when it's genuinely given and expressed it flourishes. Be a part of and enjoy the family celebrations and social events that April brings.

Your best responses for April
- Give your advice, but rest easy if it is not taken.
- Showcase the beautiful side of family and your part in it.
- Give of yourself, be generous – softly.
- Listen more, and force your opinion not at all.
- Let your humanitarian side shine.

May in a TWO Personal Year Cycle

The feeling of being in limbo may be experienced this month, as you wonder about the future while reminiscing about events that have shaped the past. Your anxiety will be much eased if you can stop analysing situations that you have no control over. Take heart, for as time moves on many things will adjust themselves and come together far better than you expected. Life is encouraging you, perhaps at times even pushing you, to look within yourself for the answers. It's an introspective kind of month, so open yourself up to the possibilities, as you ponder the questions and concerns that fill your mind. This has to do more with the actions and interactions of others, which have created outcomes you may not be happy about. Take care here as this is not a time for you to give into the resentment you may be feeling. Stop for a moment, look deeper and ask yourself whether you are expecting much more from yourself than you can possibly give. Give yourself some time out to recharge your batteries, be kind to yourself.

May is a good time to rest and recuperate from life's hectic pace. Avoid taxing your emotional health. Take time to meditate, to read or to do something else which brings you tranquillity. This is not the best time for you to demand or to insist on your rights and wants. It almost feels like nobody's listening, so pull back. Draw on your inner reserves for strength and direction and you will be surprised at how much you will gain by this month's end. Your happiness hormones are stuck in challenge mode, all the more reason to deliberately do something for no other reason than the joy it brings you. May is a great time to study or perfect something you love or need to do.

Your best responses for May
- Be selective with whom you spend your time.
- Be an observer, step outside yourself and watch your responses.
- Communicate clearly, without accusation or ultra-sensitivity.
- Conserve your energy for what matters.
- Skip the emotional comeback, take it up a notch – respond from your wisdom base.

June in a TWO Personal Year Cycle

This month is intended for some serious improvements, along with a more settled frame of mind. You can relax a little as things start to come together now. Much can be achieved through the help and support of others, so look around and see who's there for you. June is not a solo kind of month. Are you planning to do some work around the house, or on a property you manage? Perhaps some repair work, renovations or refurbishments? It might only be something minor. Organisation is needed and working to a plan will help. Utilise the mind control that June offers. Successful outcomes can come about when you are more reasonable and logical in your considerations – being emotionally driven will bring far less success. Sometimes we like to keep things under wraps and not share our ideas with others. Maybe you want to keep certain things to yourself as you wait for the best opportunity to divulge what you know, and that's OK. Family commitments may feel a little heavy, but even so, responsibilities are best met with understanding and consideration. Be supportive of the needs of others – this is not a time for selfishness, but nor is it a time for you to feel burdened. Share the load.

You will feel a sense of security as things start to come together. Be flexible in your outlook and, if warranted, seek professional help. It makes good sense to know what you are capable of and to get help with what you don't know or what may be too much for you to handle.

With so much to do the drive to accomplish may be greater than usual. For this reason, look after your health as May tests your strength and comeback ability. Issues come up that press for your time and for you to look at realistically, with your head more than your heart. And … if you want that much-deserved holiday you might have to mix business with pleasure.

Your best responses for June
- Good judgement is needed to keep your affairs in order.
- Balancing rest with work will help you achieve your targets.
- A sure and steady pace will win over a rush to the finish.
- Be strong, be resilient, but not brittle.
- Enjoy the recognition.

July in a TWO Personal Year Cycle

There's an opportunity to bring something to a conclusion this month. It may even engender a feeling of release. This is a month of change. Emotions rule, with some incident even bringing feelings of anger and/ or frustration. Life sometimes takes a hand and introduces changes in our lives to push us towards new experiences that we would otherwise be reluctant to take. The ending scripted may be from the actions of another. Nonetheless, compassion and understanding are needed now, allowing the inevitable to pass. The freedom to move about, to do what you want when you want, is not on offer. This means if you want to travel or make changes yourself, you will need to initiate and make it happen. Do not allow feelings of impulsiveness and restlessness to upset your good works. Channel any restlessness into productive activity that serves you rather than hinders you.

July is not short on drama, and if it's not yours then you'll be involved in someone else's and not essentially because you asked for it. You cannot change another person. Accept that you played your part to the best of your ability and refuse to linger in a state of 'what ifs'. Shift your mind to a more tranquil mode. Tie up any loose ends and allow the process to reach a conclusion. Be prepared as July gives your forgiveness, understanding and compassion hormones a good workout. You might want to react more forcefully, but this is your year for being cooperative and peaceful, not forceful. Your Two PYC is about promoting peaceful coexistence with those in your life. Enjoy the celebrations and social events. Give of your love without strings attached and without asking what's in it for you. What we give may not return from the person to whom we have given it. But for sure it shall return. For this reason, it's in our best interest to give only of our best. Do that.

Your best responses for July
- Let it be … with love.
- Clear any clutter and tie up any lose ends.
- Avoid losing yourself in the dramatic.
- Your energy levels are low; rest up.
- Work and achieve within the parameters Life has determined for you at this time.

August in a TWO Personal Year Cycle

You will have the feeling that something is off to a good start this month, and yet at the same time find yourself going nowhere fast. This is mainly due to the interference of others, including what they may be expecting from you. Family responsibilities may feel a little heavy during August. Some people in your life may ask for your help. At times you may think that what they are asking of you, what they expect from you, is holding you back. Caring and doing what we can for those we love is one thing, but when care moves into over-care, that's when we begin feel the weight on our shoulders. Draw the line as to what you can comfortably give and do before you move into the negative territory of feeling unappreciated. Be aware of what you say, even if you feel you are right and that you know what's best. You will be loved and appreciated when you justify less and compliment more.

Understand that this is a slow moving year, with the need for patience and faith on your part. Accept that time is needed to work things out and time is also needed for things to work themselves out. Before the month's end however, you will come to accept an idea or concept and begin to put plans into place towards making it a reality. Use the courage August both offers and tests you for to help you move forward with confidence and security in mind for the future. A sense of the spiritual, a feeling of light and wisdom will slowly infuse your being in a way that cannot discount that higher level of awareness. That level of awareness which can only be felt when the spiritual is in tune with the material. Allow yourself to go with this as it guides you towards the new in relationships and creative ideas.

Your best responses for August
- Be assertive but not aggressive.
- Take charge of your life and your decisions.
- Use some of the ideas swirling around in your mind.
- Take the lead, you have the floor.
- See family members as individuals first, as family second.

September in a TWO Personal Year Cycle

The opportunity to enjoy social and cultural events in the company of friends and loved ones will be prominent this month. September is the high point of your Two PYC, as it culminates in its very purpose of living in a peaceful, tactful and diplomatic way. And yet, do not be surprised to experience a degree of turbulence as these very qualities are put to the test. Understand that any relationship hiccup is intended to give you a practice run in responding from the very best of this year's intent – polishing and honing your ability to relate with those in your life harmoniously, lovingly and tactfully.

There is a sense of introspection which, if allowed, can take you too far inward and result in low moods. There's a chance that you discover something, or something might be brought to your attention that you wish had not been shared with you. Understand that we cannot undo the past, ours or anyone else's. Life asks you to let it be, to rise above it and move ahead. Giving in to low moods can stop you from achieving your goals, from being who you were born to be. Perhaps you feel that you have not been assertive enough and others have taken advantage of you. Or maybe you have been somewhat self-interested and others have passed you over. At times you will feel like taking control but when you do, you may discover that the outcome is not what you had anticipated.

Regardless of what you are now feeling, do not allow yourself to succumb to feeling subordinate to those in your circle. September offers you a chance to shine more brightly, so make the shift, allow yourself to feel the sensitivity that comes with the appreciation of fine art, music, aesthetics and culture. Accept people for who and what they are, even if their standards are not yours. Acceptance does not mean approval. Enjoy the social interaction of the month.

Your best responses for September
- Knowing when to step up and when to step aside will win for you.
- Trim, cut or strengthen relationships.
- Rise above the ordinary.
- Avoid rushing to respond.
- Confidentiality is a must.

October in a TWO Personal Year Cycle

The progress of your relationships carries a less intense energy this month. This in turn encourages a more positive and easy going attitude on your part. October invites you to express what you feel and what you think in ways that bring happiness to those around you as well as yourself. Your sense of authority and control sits in challenge mode, so more effort will be needed if you wish to stand up and be noticed in that way. And with an element of extravagance running through the month, be sure to know what you can comfortably spend before you flash your cash or plastic.

Friendships take centre stage and Life asks you to take time for real friends. Express your feelings gracefully and be aware of how you communicate your words and body language. Gossip is cheap during October, so do not allow yourself to be tripped up by the inclination to speak at the wrong time or through conversations that are less than integrity based. Your imagination can take you places. Use it in meditation to reinforce your good character and talents. If you do not meditate you can get the same benefits by immersing yourself, your mind, through a reverie on coming life attractions. Remember that everything starts with an idea or thought and allow only positive ones in. Someone in your life can be more pushy than nice, which may leave you feeling small. Be aware of this and refuse to be a pushover for anyone, at the same time avoiding being pushy yourself. October brings plenty of social activities with good times to be had. Enjoy sharing your thoughts, ideas and activities with those who share your days. Children and young people add to the joy of the month. Consider a class or workshop to motivate that creative energy which this month offers. Don't be surprised by the admiration that comes your way. A touch of romance could have you feeling light-headed.

Your best responses for October
- Be more enthusiastic than serious, more creative than methodical and structured.
- Be optimistic when things don't go as you would like.
- Let the child within enjoy life more.
- Express yourself in ways that work for you, not against you.
- Add a touch of creative flair to all you do.

November in a TWO Personal Year Cycle

November brings the more practical stuff of life to be taken care of. Here, it's your willingness, or not, that will determine whether the opportunities of your Two PYC are to reach maturity. The energy of the month will have you feeling more security conscious; questioning your security status in love, in career, in finances and other areas of your life. Your best approach is to buckle under to the routine and self-discipline which are now needed. Be aware that what you do this month will have an impact on the progress that is possible next year.

You may be forgiven for feeling like a ship without a rudder during November, but this does not give you a pass for frivolity. It is a time which asks you to look at people, situations and circumstances with a sense of realism. It's about seeing things as they are, as opposed to how you wish they were. Look for the facts rather than relying on sentiment alone. You might feel justified in digging in your heels in response to some of the month's happenings, but it is not an attitude that will have you achieving what you want. This is a work month, one when the practical supersedes the wish list. When you are willing to roll up your sleeves you will get so much done. It's a month geared towards getting everything on that 'to do' list ticked off. Work with others and be more obliging than testy. Finances can be a little tight this month and money is best spent on life's necessities before anything else. Family members could well be a part of your responsibilities. There are domestic and work commitments to be met but also family celebrations. Work with others if necessary to lighten the work hours. It's important that you attend to any documents in a businesslike way. Don't push yourself to overdo. Take time to look after your health and avoid getting stressed over what others are not doing, or not doing adequately.

Your best responses for November
- Be practical more than optimistic.
- If it's important, get it in writing.
- Avoid saying yes to more just because you can.
- Be organised and methodical.
- Make the most of what is available to you.

December in a TWO Personal Year Cycle

December promises to be an exciting month with more social interaction and the chance to meet friends or associates you may not have seen for some time. Feelings can be both exhilarating and confident, promoting a boost in energy. You may want to make a change or two regarding what you have planned to do this month. This can extend to changes in anticipation for added improvements you have idling in hatching mode for the coming year. Expect to do more moving around than settling down this month. This may also include travel abroad or interstate, depending on where you are along Life's continuum. December's energy can have you wanting others to see things your way. This can have you in a defensive mood when something doesn't go as you would like, or when others simply do not understand. There's a restlessness here which must not be permitted to upset the good work you have already accomplished. Better to respond than react.

Be aware that you are not in a state of mind to suffer fools easily; giving yourself a bit of space when someone presses your buttons in ways you do not like can make a difference. Be flexible and accept that others may not see what you see or may even be incapable of doing so. Remember that getting on with those in your life and resolving misunderstandings in an amicable way is the underlying mastery of your Two PYC. Help out where you can but do it in a way that engenders independence. This allows you to offer your support without taking on added responsibility. It also opens you up to the freedom the month offers. Maintain your energy and health by taking time to relax. Good times are there to be enjoyed, so don't hold back. The Christmas season this year will be energy packed.

Your best responses for December
- Be prepared for a few changes.
- Be flexible.
- Enjoy the variety of people connection.
- Let your hair down, loosen up a little.
- Agree to disagree, it's what confident and mature beings do.

Three
Personal Year Cycle

The THREE Personal Year Cycle brings experiences intended to hone and polish the following qualities and areas of life –

Joy, Sensing the Unseen, Emotion, Vision, Optimism, Communication, Inspiration, Imagination, Self-expression, Creative and Artistic Talent, Friendship, Social Interaction.

Its mandate is to prompt, encourage and at times push you to live these qualities to the very best of your ability in positive mode, and in so doing promote and sustain a constant state of evolving and becoming the whole and truly unique person you were born to be.

The THREE Personal Year Cycle

This year is about you; it is your year for self-expression. Use what inspires your creative thinking and imagination to get you where you want to go. You will feel a strong desire for self-improvement – follow your dreams, pursue the idea, but do not ignore good sense. Remember that self-improvement does not mean self-importance. Do not abandon decorum and graciousness in your quest for fun. This applies as much to men as it does women. Use the sensitivity prominent this year to connect with others in an empowering and joyful way. Refuse to allow it to become ultra-sensitivity and stop you taking a step up the ladder of success and happiness. Be on the alert for anyone trying to sweet-talk you for their own benefit. Falling for flattery or false praise can dampen the joy and prosperity the year offers. Think about what in your life you want to better. What do you want to improve? Your mind? Your body? A skill? Your choices will depend on where you are on Life's continuum. But one thing that's essentially good at every stage is nurturing your body with simple fresh quality food. For sure, you are worth the time it takes to prepare nutritious meals. For sure, you are worth determining that what you consume does not diminish but enhances your good health and wellbeing.

Joy, happiness, creativity, fun times and prosperity are the intention of the Three PYC. Your degree of happiness however, will depend on how and in what situations you demonstrate your feelings and emotions. The Three PYC is governed by senses and emotion. Our emotions can express both ends of the emotional spectrum – varying degrees between joy and sadness. When we experience what we don't want our bliss can take a dive. It is during such times that the optimism so much a part of this year's intended mastery needs to be taken on board and encouraged. Is this not when optimism is needed, when things can be more cloudy than sunny? Choose to be optimistic and happy and get your imagination working to produce where you want to be, what you desire for yourself. Understand though, that optimism does not ignore reality. Face what is and then be optimistic in your plans and strategies to optimise what is beneficial and minimise what is not.

Avoid getting drawn into situations or relationships that have you sacrificing yourself and depleting your reserves. Visualise what you want in your life. In this way you can set the pace for these things to materialise and become a reality. Align yourself with this year's requirements and you will find that by the end of your Three PYC much of what had seemed impossible is accomplished, giving you a feeling of satisfaction and fulfilment. Use common courtesy, be considerate, and listen to the advice others give you, then make your own decisions based on what is available to you. Consider the facts but be also guided by your intuition. Friends are particularly important, as is also you being a friend. The way you use your words can be power-packed this year – they have the potential to make or lose friends for you, so be aware. If you are at a stage in life where you feel comfortable without the need to make changes, then simply enjoy the year, have fun and share your optimism with those around you. This is a year for inspiring those in your life by showcasing your good character as well as your talents. You may feel a sense of youthful abandon – romance is in the air! Enjoy the social encounters the year intends for you, always with sincerity and discretion.

Your best response during a THREE Personal Year Cycle
- If there is something you wish to improve about yourself, consider it now.
- Allow the child within expression, through laughter, tears and sheer joy.
- Do something for no other reason that the joy it brings you or another.
- Be creative, intellectually, emotionally, physically – you choose.
- Be optimistic when something or someone trips you up.
- Reflect light, leave any heaviness out the door.

- Be creative in your work, including in solving problems.
- Envision where you want to be and who you want with you.
- Connect to that Higher Power and sense Its guidance.
- Buy yourself a gift that makes you happy, within your budget of course.

January in a THREE Personal Year Cycle

The beginning of this year kicks off with an air for work and all things practical. It's a month when keeping your feet on the ground will serve you best. Though the Three PYC reflects inspiration and creativity, this month's energy is geared more towards practical and domestic matters. This does not mean you cannot enjoy a January vacation, just that you will have to deliberately plan for it and then be prepared to also do what is required. It's understandable that you might want to push some things in the 'to do later' compartment of your mind, but attending to them now means you will not be adding them to next month's agenda. January's demands and requests, whether you consider them appealing or mundane, will pave the way for future benefits. Knowing this will hopefully make you more willing. Better planning and management will ensure more stability and financial security.

If you must dig your heels in about something, let it be to not allow others to upset you. Your sensitivity in response to what others say or do is on alert this month. Think clearly before responding to avoid quarrels and arguments that may cause regret later. Play your part without getting stuck on what you don't like. Your help is in demand and while it can be tiring, it's best to oblige with an open heart rather than as a chore you cannot escape. Feeling hemmed in as others create situations you would prefer to avoid can be a reality. But when you use the creative flair offered this year, you will be able to take care of what's pressing, as well as slotting in social outings with loved ones. This way, you can have your cake and eat it too, as they say. Avoid taking things too personally – in other words, lighten up!

Your best responses for January
- A month to be both sensitive and sensible.
- Attend to family matters with maturity, logic and gentleness.
- Ask others to help out where possible.
- Be more of a manager than a workhorse.
- Enjoy spending time with people you like and tolerate those you do not.

February in a THREE Personal Year Cycle

Throughout February you may be tempted to say more than you normally would. Expression through speech and the written word is encouraged this year. In light of this it's important to remember that your right to say what you feel, your freedom of speech and action does not come at the expense of other people's rights. Take care to not say something that turns away the people you want to impress or to whom you have given a little piece of your heart and which could later create regret. How you communicate your intentions can step you up or bring you down, so put some effort into this, make it deliver for you in the best ways possible. This is a busy month which includes interaction with others – socially and in business. Be alert to any opportunities and consider them in your plans for moving towards progress.

Expect Life to bring a change or two intended to polish up your flexibility and resourcefulness. Deal with any restlessness when things do not move at your pace or when you find yourself attending to boring or tedious tasks. This month carries the tendency to have you fast off the mark, so it would be wise to apply the rule 'if you can't say something nice, don't say anything at all'. Note that during February the controls are not totally in your hands. Avoid acting on feelings of anger or aggression towards anyone who antagonises you. Express your emotions in a positive way. A session with the punching bag may prove good therapy for alleviating frustrations, as pent-up emotions could lead to illness. Expect lots of activity geared towards future expectations. February being a month where anything can happen may have you changing your mind about how you want things to be. This is a time when your versatility and flexibility will aid you as you try hard to maintain your independence and your right to think and act according to your standards and beliefs. The social aspect of the month is intended for good times to be enjoyed.

Your best responses for February
- Be prepared for surprises.
- Take charge – of yourself.
- Be open to what others offer you.
- Be both resourceful and flexible.
- Enjoy the buzz in February's energy.

March in a THREE Personal Year Cycle

March asks that you prepare to be the person others depend on rather than the other way around. Choose to be the humanitarian rather than feeling imposed upon for what others expect from you. And refuse to feel like you're losing out here, as it is in this way that you will gain this month. Meet any issues with a willingness to resolve and accept any responsibilities that surface. It is not a good idea to tell those in your life how things should be or where they have gone wrong, though you might have a strong desire to do so. Shift your focus to something they are doing that is more positive than negative and commend them. View any changes with consideration for all involved. Whatever you do, even if you decide to break a relationship, do so with understanding and integrity. When love and care are given with an open heart, love, happiness and prosperity are the reward.

March is intended to be a time when you enjoy and participate in the more beautiful aspects of family, so do that. Bring flowers or something else of beauty into your favourite space. Fix things that are broken. Invite those close to you for dinner or coffee. Bake a cake and visit someone. This is not intended to be hard work. Make it a love thing rather than a duty thing and you will be rewarded in more ways than you think. Pay any outstanding accounts and be OK with being able to do so. A gracious and grateful attitude means you can move forward with certainty and security. March can be an intensely emotional month, which can result in illness if taken negatively or selfishly. An all or nothing undercurrent runs through the month so take care to think things out before acting on them. This is your month to care for others as well as yourself. Play your cards right and come out a winner!

Your best responses for March
- Enjoy family and community involvement.
- Be grateful for the chance to help someone.
- Take time to bring family together in harmony and fun.
- Listen more, insist less.
- Avoid jumping in, wait until your advice is requested.

April in a THREE Personal Year Cycle

April is not the time for you to force your views or way of thinking on anyone. You will gain more by going more with the flow of things rather than pulling against them. Those in your life may seem somewhat inattentive, so do not allow yourself to go into overdrive in an effort to get your point across or to convince someone to see what you see. If it's important to you, keep it in your heart space. Allow any ideas time to mature. You may experience hurt feelings over what others have said or done to you. Even though a part of you would like to give them a piece of your mind, April's numbers recommend that you be the wise one, the understanding one. You won't gain by overreacting. Do, of course, maintain your independence and the right to make your own decisions, but abstain from attempting to exert these ways on anyone else. Insisting on doing so could end with the loss of a friend.

Understand that what you think during April is far more important than what you do. Take time out to rest; your energy levels are lower than you might think. Relax at your favourite place, somewhere that is peaceful and serene. Take a holiday, but if your commitments do not allow that, then indulge in a massage, a movie or something else that will lighten your mood. You might catch yourself making plans to fix or improve some personal aspect of your life– enjoy that. Stay positive and choose to immerse yourself in a deep relationship with your mind and beyond. As time moves on you will see the benefit of this month's intention for quiet solitude, peace and 'blowing with the wind', as the song goes. It is not necessary to explain yourself to anyone; keep your own counsel during April and be choosy in whom you confide.

Your best responses for April

- Choose a talent you have and skill it to the max.
- Do more introspective things.
- Ask the big questions as you look up at the starry night sky.
- Observe more, especially before responding.
- Spend time with someone special, someone who wants what you want for you.

May in a THREE Personal Year Cycle

There's an undeniable feeling of confidence this month. At the same time, expect your confidence, strength and resilience to get a workout. Shape up on the inside as well as the outside. Stick to nutritious meals, move around a little, walk, dance, swim, meditate – make it enjoyable and sociable. It's important that you maintain good health and wellbeing. This will be a busy month, so take charge of things now. New directions for business and/or career are on the horizon. There's something connected to property, yours or someone else's – in your mind if not in actuality. Be sure that any important improvements take priority. Leave exaggerated optimism out the door. Be sensibly confident as well as cooperative, should you find yourself negotiating work or business conditions.

Efficiency and an executive approach are what's needed now. Use good judgement in making any important decisions, looking at both sides of the situation. Your future depends on this. Avoid being too emotional or, at the other extreme, insensitive. This is not the time for you to let your emotions rule. This month it must be your head that rules your heart if you are to take advantage of what Life offers. There is money to be paid out, but there's no need for concern, you have it for what is needed. Sensitivity could play with your heart as you ponder what you should or should not have done. Go easy on yourself and accept that perfection is not a human trait. To be perfect as a human means to do and give of your best. Be realistic and understand that you need help from others, talk to someone who knows and cares. Health issues may arise, be kind to yourself. Balance is important this month – in all that you do. Maintain self-control and be guided by your wisdom, in this way you cannot lose!

Your best responses for May
- Look confident, be confident, and back it with wisdom.
- Use gentleness to temper any harshness. It will open doors.
- Be business minded, not foolish.
- Consider every option available to you.
- Don't be the victim of smooth talkers.

June in a THREE Personal Year Cycle

Something is set to reach a conclusion this month. This may be a task or project that you have been working on, or it could even be a relationship that changes. Understand that the finality might only be in your mind at this stage as you look ahead and envision the future possibilities. June is governed by both emotional and feeling numbers which can have you going too deep and becoming lost in emotion. Be aware of this. On one hand you can feel a sense of release as you look towards an improvement in some area of your life. This can be related to property, or work. You are wise to seek professional advice if you are uncertain about any issues which may arise. Just as importantly, be sure to conduct yourself in a businesslike manner as Life asks you look beyond the now in reaching your decision. Look ahead to what can eventuate based on your decision or response.

As the weeks pass you will take on a more positive outlook. It is not advisable to repress your emotions, or your creativity, as both need an outlet for expression. If you bottle them up, chances are they may be expressed in a negative way. Rather than allow this to happen, find something that interests you and put your energy into it, be it a sport or a hobby. You do not have to be an expert at this, you just need to let yourself go and enjoy the experience. It's paramount that you maintain an optimistic outlook during June. Your feelings can have you going down memory lane and perhaps even revisiting the 'what ifs' of life. Be sure to not linger there too long. Celebrate the joy and love you feel and want for yourself and those dearest to you. Deal with anything less than the beautiful and happy only if and when it happens, and not a moment before.

Your best responses for June
- Express your feelings and emotions constructively.
- Refuse to shift into victim mode.
- Be optimistic, imagine your life's coming attractions.
- Celebrate the good and beautiful around you and within you.
- Change or let go of something that does not bring you joy.

July in a THREE Personal Year Cycle

You would be right in sensing something new this month. Or perhaps a chance to put a new face on something already there, to put a new twist on something. Though uncertainties and feeling unsure about where you are headed can be felt, you will nonetheless sense this small beginning. You will want to be up and moving, doing your own thing, and yet in another way you feel compelled to do things for others. There's a sense of duty here, possibly towards a loved one, and you can be forgiven for asking why this has not already been taken care of.

You cannot help feeling that a certain decision will have a significant influence on your future. It may even be a new perspective, a new way of thinking. Do not rush things now, and understand that though you have made a choice, it may be some time before you see the idea evolve and take shape. Use your initiative and have the courage to do what you know to be for the best. Avoid being obstinate and dogmatic as this approach will only slow you down. Understand that interruptions can keep you from making progress, so self-discipline and time management are essential. You may feel much beckoning and yet not quite be able to bring it together, a feeling that you are doing much but unable to see results to match your effort. If this is the case, then more focus is needed on what is important now, on one thing, rather than putting your time and energy on many. Remember that self-improvement and positive self-expression are what this year is about. This is not to be interpreted as just dwelling on yourself, but on what you can do to improve yourself. Open up and join in with others in friendship and goodwill. Don't bottle up your emotions, express them with joy and generosity as you involve others in your life. Stand up and be counted, for all the right reasons. Know that you can make a difference.

Your best responses for July
- Have the courage to do what you feel is needed.
- Show initiative in all you do.
- Take the lead in what you know to be real.
- Be prepared – some things only you can do.
- Focus on what's important.

August in a THREE Personal Year Cycle

Getting on with others peacefully is basically what this month is asking, even demanding from you. But neither is Life asking you to be a 'yes' person. You may experience an unanticipated comeback which makes you realise the feelings of those who share a part of your life will have to be equally considered if you are to enjoy the best outcomes possible. Though you may not approve of the choices someone close to you is making, your concern is understandable and honourable, but do not step in unless you are asked or you see an emergency situation. There will be times during August when you will want to muscle in and speak your piece loudly. But unless you use good judgement you may upset things when your intention is to fix them. Knowing when to step forward and when to step aside will win for you. Changes are scripted for the month, some of which may come unexpectedly and may not be of your choosing, but there is also opportunity for you to make a change, though you will have to initiate it. Your time may be given to details connected to the affairs of others as much as to your own.

If you wish to distance yourself from someone, or a situation, it is in your best interests to do so with a dose of tactful diplomacy and understanding to ensure an amicable outcome. Avoid having too many things on your plate as this could lead to no real accomplishment. Among the busyness of the month there are good times to be enjoyed, socially and in friendship with others. August is not a month for retreating into yourself but for venturing out and mixing with others. There's a spiritual element which underlies every response, so be aware and allow it to guide your every response.

Your best responses for August
- Decide if it's best to take charge or to support.
- When in doubt, wait.
- Be social, accept invitations.
- Relax more, join with others rather than going it alone.
- Avoid frustration, instead step back and see the opportunities that others miss. They could be for you.

September in a THREE Personal Year Cycle

There are times during September when you feel so much is expected from you that it's difficult to enjoy the simple pleasures of life. This can stir the emotions to express a combination of joy and sadness. Keep in mind that what you communicate to those in your circle will have an impact, so remember this and think before you speak, regardless of what 'they' say. It's a month governed by emotion, so take care that you do not upset yourself over other people's actions or careless words. For your part, try to contain any negative emotions. If you need to, distance yourself from negative people or situations. Life intends September to be more happy than unhappy. Part of the month will see you making plans for the future. Work on that, use your creative thinking and imagination to keep things kicking along. You can see an opportunity here that requires optimism and vision as well as responsible realism to get it to the next level. Success is possible, but you will have to go after it. Waiting for it to come to you, won't cut it and you might miss out. Be sure to get professional help if and where it is needed. This will hopefully provide the impetus you need to get out of your comfort zone and encourage you to go after what you want.

There's an element of pride running through September of which you may not be aware. It may prompt you to convince others that you know what's best or to accuse them of not doing things right. Refrain from doing either. Get back into your own life and ask yourself if you are happy with your own plans and progress. Maintain your focus here and know that it's OK to enjoy the satisfaction of having accomplished things in spite of the obstacles. Be sociable, enjoy the company of artistic and creative broadminded people.

Your best responses for September
- Express your feelings with grace.
- Do something that makes you happy.
- Spend time with those who care for you, and about you.
- Dream a few more dreams.
- Tell those in your life how much you appreciate them.

October in a THREE Personal Year Cycle

The practical and economic aspects of life will take precedence this month. October brings a need which can best be met when you assume a degree of control. It's time to organise your life and your space; bring some stability to the various aspects of what is being asked of you rather than trying to juggle them. Time management is paramount and essential if you are to accomplish what is necessary and what you want to do. Also, was your spending more liberal last month? Not a good idea this month. It's time to take a realistic look at your financial situation. Be sure to close up any gaps that leak unnecessary expenditure. October is a month for spending on life's necessities, not its wants. Consider any business agreements like a true executive as you cut and trim so you can once more be at the controls to build for the future. Make the necessary adjustments now and you won't need to concern yourself later.

Family matters may require your assistance, and though your time and energy is in high demand, do not overlook your need to rest. Do all you can but avoid taking on so much that you cannot see the wood for the trees. Sensitivity is on alert during October, including yours. Kindness and consideration for yourself as well as for those who share your days need to be factored into every response. Be understanding when someone pushes your buttons in a way that makes you feel more retaliatory than peaceful. You may find yourself reacting in regard to what others say to you or, for that matter, even what they do not say to you. Do your best to remain detached from such situations that can leave you feeling vulnerable and small. Though this is a busy month it is also intended to include the enjoyment of social outings spent with friends and family.

Your best responses for October
- Stand your ground without digging in your heels.
- A family matter can feel a little heavy.
- Take the controls but avoid being controlling.
- Be sensitive not brash.
- Include others in the situation and seek assistance.

November in a THREE Personal Year Cycle

On one hand November brings a sense of light abandon amidst much activity as you enjoy getting together with old friends and the introduction of new ones. Mixing with people from diverse backgrounds is a real possibility. It's a busy time and you will have more than one thing happening to keep you on your toes. It's a month which brings change and a feeling that some things are out of your control. Don't worry if some things are left undone, perhaps you have taken on more than you can comfortably manage. Do not be reluctant to take charge of the situation that presents itself. Someone needs to do it and if you can do it for the right reasons then go ahead. Expect the unexpected and deal with surprise situations as they arise, even if maintaining your composure proves difficult. Decisions will need to be made, so talk it over with those concerned so you can arrive at the best possible results, keeping those who matter on board. This is not just your concern. Consider opting for choices that bring improvement. Understand that you do not have to take all the responsibility on board, share it with those involved.

If you are not sure about your intentions do not allow others to overpower you with their assumptions or forceful behaviour. At the same time, make sure you yourself do not become unduly wilful when others do not see what you see. Once you have arrived at your decision adopt an attitude of courage as you push things through to a completion. Use your initiative and be resourceful. Be more flexible than rigid as you move ahead with confidence and anticipation. There is an opportunity present which has the potential to move your career forward. Take a look, perhaps it's more doable than you think.

Your best responses for November
- Be open to change, it's inevitable this month.
- Avoid going around in circles, take charge.
- Don't exclude others, let them know what's happening.
- Just because you can do it doesn't mean you cannot ask for help.
- Be flexible and consider all options available.

December in a THREE Personal Year Cycle

December brings family matters up close and personal. You may feel much is placed upon you in the way of responsibilities and obligations. Accept what is expected of you with a light and willing heart. You're right in thinking there won't be much free time for yourself, however you will be grateful for the special time spent in the company of those you love. The month brings an opportunity for you to care for someone and though you may wonder how you will manage, see it as a chance to go beyond yourself.

It is understandable to feel used when others expect so much from you or when you think that others are shirking their share of responsibilities. You may be right in feeling that you are doing more than some. But in all this it pays to remember that December is your turn to serve others. You are the one someone close is relying on for support. Do this with an open heart and you will be rewarded for your generosity and through what you do. This is not the time for you to be selfish. Life intends for you to focus more on the love and happiness given and received than anything else. This can be a most beautiful and memorable time, but only when you shift your attention to making others happy. Delight in the beauty and warmth of the people in your life at this time and enjoy the success that comes your way. Be sure to take the time to show those that hold a little piece of your heart just how much you love them and how grateful you are to have them in your life. Enjoy your home and its surroundings, appreciate all you love about it and the comfort it brings you. Add your own personal touches, if only for the sheer pleasure they bring you. Enjoy the festivities as you celebrate the Christmas season in your own special way.

Your best responses for December

- Shift your attention to the beautiful of life.
- Appreciate the rewards that come with caring for others.
- Be gracious.
- Although difficult at times, look for the good.
- Celebrate family – all of it.

Four
Personal Year Cycle

The FOUR Personal Year Cycle brings experiences intended to hone and polish the following qualities and areas of life –

Practicality, Willpower, Grounding, Management, Construction, Reliability, Application of Science and Maths, Seriousness, Family Duty, Relating Facts, Organisation, Structure.

Its mandate is to prompt, encourage and at times push you to live these qualities to the very best of your ability in positive mode, and in so doing promote and sustain a constant state of evolving and becoming the whole and truly unique person you were born to be.

The FOUR Personal Year Cycle

The theme for this year is work. There's no mistaking the energy carried during this cycle, in which all things practical take precedence. A year when reality and not pretence is the norm and what will win for you. It is a year for doing and for accomplishing. It is not a year for daydreaming or for haphazard adventure. Look at it for what it offers you – a time for you to build, whether a house, a family, a career, a business, a relationship. Based on sound principles, practical values and constant application, according to where you are on Life's continuum. Take off your roller skates and be prepared to advance as the turtle rather than as the hare. It will require determination and perseverance. Life will encourage, expect and at times push you to be more organised and to bring more structure to all you do. If you are prepared to do this, if you can deliver, then you will be amply rewarded.

Your Four PYC will expect you to manage your affairs and finances with efficiency and discipline. You may notice money going out, just be sure it goes where it can benefit you. Make no mistake, this is a year when you start laying the foundations for the security and stability that is possible for the future. Its requirements cannot be skipped or passed over. To do so would be to deny yourself the satisfaction that comes with success and achievement. If you feel restricted or confined, accept this and make the most with what you have available to you. Restriction is part of the energy of the year. The intention behind it is to encourage you to work within limitations, to stick to the task at hand until it's completed in order to ensure sound results. Success will come through self-discipline, commitment, determination, perseverance and attention to details.

It is time to get real with where you are in your life. Look at your circumstances, your life and those in it, with stark realism. For what is. For who and what they are. Write down everything you own and every amount you owe. In other words, make a list of your assets and liabilities. Your business and personal assets should be considered in an economic sense in order for you to know what your base is for future growth and direction. When you discipline yourself to do this, you will definitely experience the satisfaction of having achieved and accomplished what you set yourself to do. This will set the background for more freedom next year.

Before you say it's all too hard, it doesn't have to be all work and no play. Social activities, outings and enjoyment are also scripted into the year's timetable. When your help is required, be gracious about it, even if you cannot understand why some people act the way they do. Let's be clear here though – being helpful and generous does not mean allowing yourself to be used. Family and all that it stands for will be in force this year and may feel more heavy than helpful. This is more a year for what needs to be done as opposed to what you desire to do. But look at it this way, if you convince yourself to do what is necessary, it will set the grounding essential for success and also free up time and resources the following year for what you want to do. This is a time for buying, selling and improvements. Be sure to read the small print before signing any documents. The year's energy reflects the physical aspect, so do not avoid getting medical attention or advice if needed. Be sure to eat well, have adequate rest and slot in anything else that induces good health and wellbeing.

Your best responses in a FOUR Personal Year Cycle
- If it's important, get it in writing.
- Be willing to do more and not less.
- Support family members, but do not carry them.
- Look at everything realistically.
- Take some of the ideas of last year and make them a reality.
- Be prepared to work within limitations.
- Accept that work comes before pleasure.
- Buy only what is essential and of good quality and substance, whether a handbag or a house.
- Make sure your hard work is paying dividends.
- Delight in what you have achieved.

January in a FOUR Personal Year Cycle

You will feel the urge to get moving with things this month and though you are keen to get things done, you are not quite sure how to set plans in motion in order to achieve the best results. There is no need to rush into things. It is more important to ensure that whatever you do will have a positive bearing on the future, so take the time to sort out what you want to do. Expect to be involved with others, whether for work reasons or in your personal life, so be aware of this and pay attention to any opportunities for improvement. With this in mind know that your plans to accomplish and your desire to get things settled may be foiled or upset by having to deal with many agendas or simply because you may need to rely on others.

Your heart-strings may be fine-tuned this month as you experience low moods intermingled with excitement and enthusiasm. Joy mixed with sadness. Dealing with others is not always easy and January is no exception. Go easy on the criticism, even though you may feel it is deserved. Do not allow your sensitivity to other people's arrogance to upset you or to break up a friendship you think is worth salvaging. Pay close attention to your health this month and do not avoid taking care of yourself with the excuse of having no time or believing that it will take care of itself. Avoid slipping too far in negative territory. Do something simply for the sheer joy it brings you to lift your moods back into positive ground. As the month progresses, uncertainty and nervousness will give way to clarity of mind. Change, a trip perhaps, social activities and family responsibilities are all part of this month's energy.

Your best responses for January
- With your communication channel in challenge mode, keep your words positive.
- Avoid forcing your opinion on others.
- Enjoy the people interaction.
- Look for opportunities to shine a little brighter.
- Be more like a flexible willow than a rigid pine.

February in a FOUR Personal Year Cycle

February has you off the mark with lots to do. Much of this will be in practical areas having to do with the home and family as well as work related. But take heart, for without a doubt, as your stress levels decrease your energy levels will increase. It's easy to give in to hurt feelings if you yourself pump them with extra oxygen, but you cannot afford to invest your energy in low moods, you have too much to do and too many people relying on you. Consider the state of your emotions in this as this could impact on your health. If you feel overwhelmed by it all or have said 'yes' too often and over-committed your time and resources, then ask for help or delegate to others. This may be a side effect of wanting to have things settled. Know that you do not have to do it all, nor do you have to do it all now.

Spending time with your favourite people will add joy and wellbeing to your life, so do it, enjoy it, relish it! Family is factored in but it is not intended to weigh you down this month. It is more about encouraging you to express the love and gratitude for the good things that family means to you, including your place in it. If you are tempted to focus on what you don't have in your life, switch mind channels and deliberately keep in view the good that is in your life. Avoid feeling small if others are insensitive to your feelings. Be assertive if the situation calls for it but take care to not be abrasive or bombastic. Enjoy the social aspect and celebrations amidst the duties and responsibilities that are part and parcel of this month's energy.

Your best responses for February
- Appreciate the little things.
- Family matters cannot be avoided.
- You might feel justified in putting someone in their place, but don't.
- Surround yourself with those who care.
- Do what you can without feeling emotionally depleted.

March in a FOUR Personal Year Cycle

Amidst the duties and responsibilities of the year, March will give you a desire to spend more time on your own, away from the hustle and bustle of life and its many demands and expectations. This is a good time for you to take a holiday, but if this is not possible perhaps you can sneak in a weekend away somewhere. Your state of mind is important now. There may be a problem that calls for your attention, even if you are not responsible for creating it. Part of this may concern your health and it's possible that your finances are also in focus. The best action is no action unless you are absolutely certain of your intentions. Pull back a little for a clearer perspective on how things are progressing. Observe what is happening. Have a little faith and you will find that this approach will give any issues a chance to resolve themselves. Keep your own counsel and indulge in a good dose of rest and relaxation.

It is important to avoid negative moods. Your confidence in a positive outcome will go a long way in ensuring it. Going with the flow of things will see that you do not throw a spanner in the works, which could sabotage the success the year promises. You may experience opposition from others and no matter how much you try to help, it somehow comes out wrong. It can feel like you have little or no control over the matter. Do not allow this to worry you, step back and accept the situation or condition for what it is, allow others to have their say. If this is someone else's issue, release it and remind yourself that you can accomplish despite the problems. You may consider selling something in order to bring about an improvement. Give it some thought if you believe it to be worthwhile. Use your wisdom and tackle issues on an intellectual level with executive skills and wisdom, but not with emotion.

Your best responses for March
- Go with the flow of Life, rather than resist.
- It's a month for receiving and accepting, not for going after.
- Spend time alone and be intuitively guided.
- Not a time to start something new, but for perfecting something already in operation.
- Say less, observe more, study, research and question.

April in a FOUR Personal Year Cycle

You will feel more control and willpower with less emotional vulnerability this month. This is a good time to put things in motion for buying, selling, renovating, fixing – in your mind space if not actually doing it. Expect discussion to come up in regards to property matters. Whatever business plans you have been nurturing, April is the month to move with them in order to maximise their potential success and financial improvement. Consider your options so you can take the next step, however small. You will feel a certain satisfaction as you see your plans start to show results. Good management and a composed attitude will serve you well now. Your strength and resilience will be tested, so make time for much-needed rest and relaxation if you feel as though you are on a treadmill, with so much requiring your attention. Your thoughts seem to accompany your determination to get things done. It's like being on a mission to accomplish, as you direct your affairs towards more stability and improvement. Careful management of finances will ensure that you do not over-estimate your budget or your net worth.

Wisdom is needed now. Understand there are no shortcuts in avoiding the constant effort required if you are to achieve the results you want. Do not allow the setbacks that others create to stop you from moving forward to ensure security, even though it may seem to be at snail's pace. This is an all or nothing month, so refrain from leaving things to chance. Read all documents and be certain that you understand them before signing. In this way you will not be committing to anything without complete awareness as to what you are agreeing to. Sound judgement in your affairs and executive ability will allow you to see an improvement even if there is still much to be taken care of.

Your best responses for April
- Balance will ensure you don't overdo things.
- Be strong, but not brittle.
- Get the full picture before making important decisions.
- Be as a judge – fair and just in all you do.
- Enjoy the authority and recognition – make both work for you.

May in a FOUR Personal Year Cycle

May is a good month for completing any unfinished business. Take the opportunity to bring to completion a plan or work that has been in the making. Endings, conclusions and new decisions on the home and business front will call for your consideration. This will in turn have you looking in new directions as you consider taking up new projects. Perhaps a person or a situation, maybe a place of residence, has reached completion stage in your life. This can occur as a natural consequence of events or from choice. Stagnant situations will need to be addressed and worked through to allow new opportunities to get underway. Life is asking you to let go of what is no longer necessary for your spiritual growth or what you no longer want in your life. Or perhaps it's about accepting that someone wants to move on and allowing them the freedom and blessing to do so. Maintain objectivity and adopt an attitude of compassion, understanding and also forgiveness if needed. It's in this way that Life will reward you, if not immediately then for sure in the years ahead.

This is a good time for clearing out all those things that you have been holding on to 'just in case'. Collect what you have not used in years and have a garage sale, or give it away. Try also to let go of any emotional baggage. Bless anything or anyone you may feel regret over and release it with love. This is essential if you are to see your way forward with clarity and vision. Engage your time and resources in doing things for others, purely for the sake of helping. Understand that much is happening, even if you feel that things are at a standstill.

Your best responses for May
- Take care to not let your feelings take a dive.
- Make any decisions out of love, not fear.
- Let go of what is no longer useful.
- Refuse to get caught up in other people's dramas.
- May is for receiving, accepting, and reflecting. Not for pursuing.

June in a FOUR Personal Year Cycle

There are decisions to be made this month, which will require you to use your head more than your heart. Something might make you feel small, but Life is asking you to take the lead here. Look at the situation from a detached position, even if the matter is personal. It is in your best interest to search for the facts. Once you have made your decision be determined to stay on track. It's a busy time for you as you deal with issues and expectations that call for your attention, so it's essential that you realise your true abilities and skills. This is not the time for an inflated view of what you can and cannot do. By all means, have a vision for the future in mind, but be realistic as well as courageous and insightful. This will enable you to get that grounding for future security and improvement, not only for yourself but also for others that are involved.

Avoid being overly sensitive in your reactions to what others do or don't do. Rather, take a step back, clear your mind and be sure any decisions are justified. Remind yourself that it's not your business how others choose to live their lives. Remain confident even when others are not as supportive as you had expected. Family issues may take up some of your time, but this is unavoidable. Deal with what is apparent even if it means that the outcome will be change which was not anticipated. Keep an eye on your personal affairs and understand that finances may be a bit slow. Enjoy the sense of authority, the energy and interests that June delivers. Your health or that of a loved one is asking for attention – don't side-step it. Strive for balance and harmony and you will find that things will work out.

Your best responses for June
- Reason more, emote less.
- Courage and foresight are what's needed now.
- Refuse to allow your sensitivity to take you backwards.
- Consider others, yes, but not at your loss.
- Not a time to be in idle mode, know where you're going and gear up.

July in a FOUR Personal Year Cycle

Issues and situations arise this month to provide opportunities to practise your peacemaking qualities. Much of what you do now is in connection with others. Tact and diplomacy will win for you, but not so stubborn pride and obstinacy. If you find yourself in a mini-crisis during July, an assertive attitude blended with a dose of understanding will work best for you. When you adopt this frame of mind you will find the outcome to be far better than you had first anticipated. Meeting some of Life's experiences during July entails a big effort on your part. This is necessary so you can maintain a happy and optimistic outlook. There's a spiritual element in this month's energy which is intent on showing you that it's not what happens to you, but how you respond that carries the capacity to step you up a notch or leave you at a standstill. Look beyond the obvious. When you shift your attention to the macro of Life rather than the micro, you will see so much more than the ordinary.

July's happiness hormones are in challenge position. This means that it's up to you to make the effort to do things that make you happy. Say yes to social invitations which come from those you love. Mix with friends and family, as you come together to celebrate and remember. Be more expressive in communicating your feelings and desires, make them come from your heart space. In this way you will inspire those around you as you draw to yourself the help that you need. What others can do now is real, and perhaps more than you would care to acknowledge. July challenges you to play your part in showcasing your qualities as a peaceful negotiator and leader.

Your best responses for July
- Ask yourself whether your best move is forward or to the side.
- Avoid worrying about what others do.
- Express your emotions in joy, not criticism or pride.
- Take the lead but be sure it includes others' wellbeing.
- Know who are your friends and who are acquaintances.

August in a FOUR Personal Year Cycle

You can afford a little self-indulgence this month, but take care to not totally lose yourself in idle conversation, as what you say throughout August carries weight. How you express your emotions, in speech or in other ways, has the potential to advance or retard your efforts – so choose your words carefully, make them work for you and not against you. Gardening, writing, assignments, painting, fine cooking or any other activity will get your creative juices flowing and gives you a sense of accomplishment and wellbeing. Many of the ideas you have been turning over in your mind can now be taken to the next level. Be optimistic without being overly so, as you look for ways to give birth to your plans. Be sure to do what is necessary. This is not about shirking your commitments, but about organising your time to do what is necessary as well as making time for pleasure and enjoyment with friends and special others. Savour the enthusiasm and then let it spur you on to make some of those ideas, some of those dreams, a reality.

Understand that all is well as you give situations and opportunities a chance to progress to the next stage of development. There is work demanding your attention which has the potential to add security and financial improvement in your life, but you must do the work. Family and responsibilities might feel more on the heavy side as your heart is geared towards the lighter side of life. This is an excellent time for a holiday, so get your bags packed and invite someone you love to share the experience. Money should be there for you as a result of past efforts. Spend some of it and have yourself a ball without being extravagant.

Your best responses for August
- Have yourself some fun.
- Add a touch of the creative to all you do.
- Do not be careless with your affection.
- Be aware that you do not undo your past good works.
- Envision where you want Life to take you.

September in a FOUR Personal Year Cycle

You may feel somewhat restricted as this month's energy takes hold. If you get the feeling that you are not as free as you would like, you're right. There's something holding you back, restricting your ability to get around your way. Avoid feeling walled in. Life is expecting you to work within the context of what is available to you and what you yourself are capable of doing. Understand that your Four PYC is encouraging and perhaps at times even forcing you to act on your plans. To get things done. This will offer you more freedom next month. September is a time for attending to the practical side of life – doing things that may feel more mundane than inspiring. The work that presses for your time, however, must be done. Duties, obligations and expectations need to be met if you are to accomplish what is necessary, what is essential to provide the security you want. When you apply yourself to meeting these expectations, satisfaction and success will eventually be gained. Remind yourself, if you must, that the result of hard work is not necessarily instantly visible. Remind yourself also of the success that you have achieved thus far.

Matters involving property, documents and health will call for your attention. Be aware of any restlessness which can put you off course and even hinder your progress. It's important that you take time out to connect socially with others. September is intended to show positive results in that business venture as you look ahead to future possibilities. You will be pleased to see your efforts starting to bear fruit, which should encourage you to keep moving forward. Avoid being critical and understand that we are all on our own path on Life's continuum. You might find yourself doing more for others this month, particularly for family and community. Do what you can without going into overload and depleting your reserves.

Your best responses for September
- Do and give of your best, nothing more is expected.
- If you want free time then you will have to make it happen.
- Enjoy the social interaction.
- Discipline yourself to do what is needed now.
- Work with others to get the results you want.

October in a FOUR Personal Year Cycle

As October gets under way you can feel a shift towards more freedom and excitement. This will be a busy month with lots to do and the promise of success nudging you forward. Changes to some of last month's decisions are intended for improvement. So be sure that any changes you make are not haphazard or made on the spur of the moment. Think them through and make certain they will improve your lot, or at the very least not undo the good work already underway. Attend to legal matters with a serious edge. Progress is the key word as you take advantage of interesting experiences and new people coming into your life, as one-off meetings or possible friendships. Add a good dose of enthusiasm to your attitude, even if the capacity to enjoy the simple pleasures of life is sometimes in the too-hard basket. Dismissing your feelings is not the way, but then neither is foolish talk. Perhaps talking to someone in whom you can confide might help you see things from a lighter perspective.

You might catch an opportunity or two, if so choose what is important to you now, with an eye to the future. Should you feel compelled to criticise what you do not approve, be sure your criticism is constructive. There is fun to be had this month so mix with young and old, different cultures and careers. Watch your cash balance as it may be a bit wanting. Avoid overspending as you get caught up in the activities of the month. Have a good time but keep your feet on the ground.

Your best responses for October
- Be a part of something that brings happiness.
- Be prepared for changes, those Life brings and those you initiate.
- Mix with people from different backgrounds.
- You may feel inclined to bend a few rules, just don't break them.
- Do not be overly concerned if you take two steps forward and one to the side. Just keep moving.

November in a FOUR Personal Year Cycle

As the year winds to a close you may well find yourself with more to do than you had anticipated. Much of this will be of a practical nature and will include family. Be prepared to be involved in the lives of others. The situation you are considering regarding an issue or someone in your life is best kept to yourself for now. An opportunity may present itself for you to take care of a loved one due to ill health or to help them meet their obligations. You may even find that money is a little tight, but this is not of great importance now. Take care of own health and try not to give into negative feelings if things are not as you would like them to be.

You may feel burdened by what is placed on your shoulders, by what is expected of you. But then again, perhaps you are expecting too much from yourself. Albeit some of this may involve preparation and obligations having to do with the Christmas season. Maybe you had not thought of the work involved in hosting Christmas lunch or dinner. Perhaps you were more focused on how beautiful it would be to have everyone together, and so it would. But it is also possible that some family members may not match your generosity and care, which can make you more sensitive to feeling unappreciated. This is not the most conducive frame of mind to adopt at this time. Know there is a lot of love around you, so you will get your share from those special to you. This is a time for family gatherings and enjoyment amidst the seriousness of duties and responsibilities. This month Life intends that you match your work schedule to your enjoyment schedule.

Your best responses for November
- Offer to be there for someone who needs you.
- Refuse to judge what's right, what's wrong or how things should be.
- Enjoy family and what you can do to showcase all that's good.
- Feeling small doesn't mean you are; avoid shifting into victim mode.
- Be willing to give and receive love and appreciation.

December in a FOUR Personal Year Cycle

As much as you might wish to blend into everything and become invisible at times, Life will expect you to participate in what's going on and appreciate your unique contribution. The Christmas season this year, though buzzing with much on the agenda, will have you yearning for quality time on your own or with a special few others. You may feel like opting out of the busyness around you and if you can manage a holiday this month, well and good, for it could be just what you need. Christmas can sometimes release hormones of the blues as the expected joy of the festive season can sometimes feel more like an emptiness. Life asks that you get your reserves from within this month as you turn to your higher self for the wisdom and understanding that will serve you well at this time.

Make time for quiet contemplation, read inspirational material – look for literature or movies that will lift your spirit. As your mind takes you on journeys into the past, try not to dwell too much on what is missing in your life. Take leisurely walks or spend quiet time in your favourite space. This may help stimulate the peace and serenity which your soul craves right now. Avoid being too dogmatic or arrogant when people rub you the wrong way. This is a good time to practise humility without the sensation of feeling humiliated. Going with the flow of things will win for you this December. If money is not free flowing, take care to not overspend, which could result in more strain than you need take on board. Enjoy Christmas for what it is, as you reflect on the events of the past year with wisdom, acceptance and understanding.

Your best responses for December
- It may be hard to keep your finger on the pulse.
- Be more relaxed than apprehensive.
- If it's not urgent, let it be for another time or for someone else.
- Say less, observe and think more.
- Socialise only with those who brighten your day.

Five
Personal Year Cycle

The FIVE Personal Year Cycle brings experiences intended to hone and polish the following qualities and areas of life –

Freedom, Progress, Change, Flexibility, Energy, Quick Thinking, Versatility, Resourcefulness, Investigation, Salesmanship and Promotion, Adventure, Curiosity.

Its mandate is to prompt, encourage and at times push you to live these qualities to the very best of your ability in positive mode, and in so doing promote and sustain a constant state of evolving and becoming the whole and truly unique person you were born to be.

The FIVE Personal Year Cycle

After meeting the practical requirements of last year, you can almost sense a heaviness lifting from your shoulders. Freedom, change and independence are keywords for this year. Not a reckless and selfish freedom – that would only undo all your hard work thus far, including past accomplishments. Life intends it to be a more productive freedom, one that brings progress and allows you live more closely to the authentic you. More than ever, you will want to think and act according to your ways, your standards. It can be a truly liberating feeling and one to be enjoyed. Just take care that what you want does not override another's needs. Do not give in when tempted to be critical of others if they do not share your bravado this year, or if they fail to see what you see. This is a year when bending the rules may not be given enough thought, so be sure to know and understand any rules you intend to bend. Ask yourself if you can handle the risk that comes with it. The daring impulse scripted into this year's energy is there to test your response to every situation during its influence.

This is a people year and much can be gained when you get out there and mix with others, socially and in business. Do not pull back from meeting and interacting with people outside your circle. Take part in community activities, entertainment, the forming of groups and even fundraising events. Get acquainted with anything that resembles a career opportunity, or even a wider social circle. It is possible that your involvement in such things can open you up to change you had not considered. Work in the public sector is intended to offer and encourage success and advancement. Anything different will excite and capture your interest this year. For sure, there are people to meet and places to go – but stand still for a moment and consider the opportunities that life is now offering you. Refuse to waste your time chasing too much and achieving next to nothing. Avoid scattering your energy and resources, make a conscious decision as to which or what is important to you now. Ask yourself what is doable now. Be realistic as well as enthusiastic and be prepared to leave what is not doable for another time.

Expect changes as old problems resolve themselves. In fact, expect the unexpected this year. Surprises will be there for you to practise and polish your flexibility and resourcefulness. When you don't get what you want, allow the dust to settle, gather your strength and then be adamant that you will get some good from the experience, whether spiritual, material or both. You might decide to break with a tradition, and that's OK, but do think about it first, don't make it a rash decision. Be patient, discreet and avoid arguments. Demonstrate versatility and flexibility in business and social interests. Spirituality will feature in your life this year, in a more personal than public way. Whatever you do be clear about any dealings that could lead to legal problems. If this year's progress is not money driven, it will be in the experience gained that will prepare the way to include money in the years ahead. Take time to care for others and you will be rewarded with inspiration and more. Use good judgement in all you do and put more zest into your life. The urge to travel will be felt in your bones. Allow yourself to enjoy the thrill and excitement that the year has in store without breaking the rules or undoing the good you have already set in place. Enjoy the new contacts, change and progress intended for the year.

Your best responses in a FIVE Personal Year Cycle
- Forget surviving, *live* your life!
- See your life not as something you have to get through, but as a grand adventure.
- Look for new opportunities to better your position.
- Look at what is already established and how you can change it for improvement.
- Mix with people from different cultures and different lines of business.
- Live out loud but not dangerously so.

- Avoid taking risks that come with a bottomless outcome.
- Travel – within your area, interstate, internationally, on the net or in your mind.
- If you get bored buy something new, just be sure it's within your budget.
- If you plan to move house or job, make it a progressive move or no move.

January in a FIVE Personal Year Cycle

Though the Five PYC is geared towards more freedom and independence, you may well find that January brings its fair share of commitments. Some of these responsibilities may have eventuated as outcomes to changes which occurred in previous years. It's important that you do your best to take care of what is pressing for your attention. You are not acting alone here, this is not just about you, and so you will need to discuss things with those involved. Doing this, acting in ways that include rather than exclude those involved, will ensure that a more harmonious agreement can be reached. Keep in mind that the outcome sought needs to benefit all concerned. When you go in with this intention any discord will be minimised, if not eliminated. Going in with a more dominant and bull headed approach will only alienate or upset those involved. Resist the temptation to pick up your boxing gloves, but do make the effort to appreciate something if not all of what others are doing, even though you would prefer things were done differently.

This is a year of change, and being flexible in your approach to people and situations will prove to be as beneficial to your own personal outcomes as to anyone else's. Rest assured, there is a plan in progress, even though you may not be aware of it. Be patient, wait for the facts to come to the surface and you will have your rewards. Family features this month – the duties, obligations and celebrations. Your help is needed, so show you care. Attend to any health matters that may arise, whether yours or another's. This is a month when patience, care and appreciating the good stuff win over strong judgements and/or egotistical pride.

Your best responses for January
- Showcase your caring side
- Enjoy the lighter side of family and be prepared to handle the sometimes heavier feel of it.
- Play it right and enjoy the success.
- Give more compliments, share the love.
- Lead by example.

February in a FIVE Personal Year Cycle

If meditation is not already a part of your daily routine, now's a good time to start. It does not need to be a meditation where you sit in lotus position. It can be taking a slow and pensive walk in nature or in a quiet suburban street. Of course you can also meditate sitting in your favourite armchair. If any thoughts come, let them float out, but do not force them out. Look after your health as worry and stress over what you feel is not right will only slow the progress of the year. Getting hot under the collar can lead to mistakes with the possibility of regret or even of renewing issues for you to deal with. Consider the present situation objectively and in light of the months ahead. Things will improve – but you must first believe in yourself.

With freedom and change in the air, take the time to consider your options with regard to future expectations. You may feel some things are at a standstill, including your finances, but hang in there and do not give way to low moods. Maintaining some degree of control over your emotions is important now. Life is asking you to respond from a higher level, that of wisdom and not emotion. Be on guard as you can take things to heart more than you would ordinarily. Your ego is at risk of going into overdrive if you allow your sensitivity to grow to out-of-proportion levels. Make it a priority to do something that makes you happy. Catch up with a friend or watch a funny movie or sitcom on television. Keep positive and allow the luck of the number seven, which is active this month, to enter into your life and bring you some much needed rewards.

Your best responses for February
- Do not allow your emotions to take a dive.
- Stand back more from the action and observe before responding.
- Not a time to create waves, build sandcastles instead.
- Look at the good in your life and be grateful for it.
- Make time for quiet thought, reflection and joy.

March in a FIVE Personal Year Cycle

March brings a sense of empowerment, even if a part of you feels somewhat vulnerable. There is an element of change running through the month which you will recognise soon enough. This could be connected to outside issues or perhaps with you more directly. Addressing this now will provide an outcome availing you opportunity and more personal freedom. You may feel more confusion than clarity and if that is so, take one step at a time and do not allow your mind to be bombarded with too much at once. Life expects you to be the strong one here, the one capable of reasoning things through logically. At the same time, you will find that the sensitivity and hesitancy you feel may be just as strong as the strength you need right now. Be aware of any opposition and meet it with an attitude of balanced judgement, looking at both sides of the situation objectively.

While you can be determined to push through with your plans, take care to approach all delays in a business-like manner. Attend to any necessary changes with proficiency and attention to details. Even if results are not forthcoming as quickly as you had anticipated, understand that in the macro of life everything is as it should be, and encourage yourself to be at ease with that. Financial improvement is on the horizon though this is not intended as a licence for extravagance. Your emotional sensitivity can be kept in positive range simply by not taking to heart anything that is said to you or about you that you do not like. March will show improvement when you manage your affairs with a business mentality and a dose of diplomacy.

Your best responses for March

- Maintain good health as your strength and resilience are given a workout.
- While sensitivity can open doors, being ultra-sensitive in your responses will close them.
- Avoid being one-sided when making decisions.
- Consider all options before responding.
- Add a dose of gentleness in your approach.

April in a FIVE Personal Year Cycle

Some situation or circumstance that has been a part of your life is projected to arrive at a climax this month. The energy around you can feel somewhat dramatic, and even if it's not your drama, you may be pulled in just the same. Be sympathetic without going too deep. Understand that how you respond to others now will affect future outcomes. Be aware as there may be some confusion or emotional upset when you realise that some aspect of the past cannot be incorporated into your plans for the future. Your part is to let it go. Look at it as Life giving you an opportunity to exercise tolerance and goodwill, along with understanding if necessary. Look at it like this because this is how it is.

We can be forgiven for sitting on the fence to avoid making the wrong decision, but your Five PYC is now asking you to climb down and take a stand for what you believe needs to be resolved. Perhaps someone is not doing the right thing. Taking control may not be the easiest thing to do, but the time has come for you to take matters into your own hands and make the necessary changes or adjustments that are now necessary. For your part, make sure the results for which you aim are fair for all involved. Avoid arguments; instead know that good discussion and honest communication of your intentions will bring more positive results. Be assertive but not selfish as you refuse to allow others to faze you. Attend to your health and to any legal matters with efficiency. There is the possibility of travel this month and of being exposed to situations and circumstances outside the usual. Be prepared as the events and goings on of the month can have your adrenalin pumping.

Your best responses for April
- Remember that love, not its opposite, makes for harmony and justice.
- Be understanding and sympathetic but do not carry another's responsibility.
- Be reasonable.
- Remember that understanding and forgiveness do not delete accountability – for you or for the other.
- Take the lead, but take your heart with you.

May in a FIVE Personal Year Cycle

It's easy for impulse to take charge when you consider the freedom and change so prominent in a Five PYC. Mind control and lateral thinking, however, are paramount now. Make your health a priority by taking time to rest, especially if you feel far too busy to do so. From a mental perspective, you should be more relaxed now because any confusion or uncertainty has begun to lift, allowing you to see more clearly. You can sense something is off to a fresh start and even your emotions have assumed a steadier tempo. Take the chance to meet new people this month and perhaps you may even detect an opportunity which will prove to be to your advantage. By all means consider what Life offers with courage and foresight for what can be.

May brings new ideas. A new perspective on something already underway, perhaps. It's a time to be confident, but in all this, understand that this is not about rushing things through. Do not be put off by someone acting in a manner which is displeasing to you, of which you do not approve. Sure, some circumstances and conditions may not be to your liking or approval, but there is nothing you cannot handle with an assertive and cool attitude. This is a month which can produce accomplishment and progress. The only thing to mar this forward-moving time is a mindset of arrogance and rigidity. Your Five PYC expects you to avail yourself to the opportunities now on offer and to consider all options before making decisions. There is an underlying current of all or nothing running through May – best to aim for the all.

Your best responses for May
- Begin by taking charge – of yourself first and foremost.
- Don't let uncertainty stop you from making progress.
- Make composure your ally.
- Make a start on understanding how this month's ideas can be used for future progress.
- Be OK with standing on your own if need be.

June in a FIVE Personal Year Cycle

The experiences Life intends to deliver to you in June require a mix of assertive and cooperative responses, if you are to benefit from its offerings. And therein lies the catch, because how can you be both these opposites, I hear you ask. Life is intent on polishing up how you interact with those in your life. The Five PYC offers you a sharpness for seeing more, so put this to use and decide when the circumstances require you to be assertive or to be cooperative. There is much that can be accomplished through tact, patience and a quiet confidence. Your determination and strength of will may be tested, so take care and refrain from coming across too strong. Life is not asking you let others walk over you, just to add a little heart to that sense of authority and being in charge. You do not want to ignite problems when your intention is for harmony.

Refuse to allow little things to annoy you or to get the better of you. First and foremost, June asks that you take control over yourself, and your stuff. Your Five PYC will test your good character to awaken you to the needs of others. Understand that it is not always in your best interest to push forward without consulting those involved, especially if it's someone close to you. Try to accept that much of what happens in our sojourn on this planet is not always visible or apparent on the surface of things. Relationships can change, and if it's in your control then make the alterations necessary to give you the change you want to see. June challenges you to be patient as well as sharp. Use your intellect and communicate your feelings with those in your life, not at them. Parties, celebrations and invitations are there for you to enjoy and to showcase your charismatic side.

Your best responses for June
- Avoid wavering, take control of your life.
- Observe before responding, is it yours to own? If not, resist giving your opinion.
- Be aware – does the situation ask you to step up or to step to the side?
- June offers you a chance to shine more brightly.
- Blend tact and gentleness with strength and authority.

July in a FIVE Personal Year Cycle

There is a joyful and inspirational influence running through the month of July – tap into it and allow yourself to be a part of it. When you blend this month with the freedom and independent influence of your Five PYC, the social aspect open to you tells you it's time to mingle, time to shift some of your focus to include a little more leisure, a little more pleasure. There's also an emotional element here, so be sure to not go overboard in displaying your feelings. Be receptive to forming new friendships and strengthening established ones. Say yes to more invitations as well as yourself doing the inviting. The energy of the month lends itself to holidaying, so if that's what you have in mind, July's less serious energy provides the encouragement you may need.

Tap into that store of inspiration and self-expression and you may find something there that has the potential to bring you both success and happiness in your life. This is not a time for you to take a back seat, as you will need to use your sense of reason and intellect as you pursue the ideas and concepts with gusto. Friends and family add to the fun and good times of the month – enjoy. Avoid being ultra-sensitive in response to anything negative that may come from others. It's important that you make a big effort to lighten your mood and not deepen it. Though July does not carry a serious tone, it can stimulate emotional reactions for sadness as well as joy. Direct your emotions towards a more positive edge and go easy on the spending, as there's an element of extravagance around. Take the opportunities that life is now offering you. Be creative and if you do nothing else, do something that makes you and someone else happy!

Your best responses for July
- Be attentive to the little things.
- If you can't say anything nice, it's best to not say anything at all.
- With sensitivity and emotions directing the month, be sure to express them graciously.
- Good communication is key; it will open doors that would otherwise be closed.
- Add courtesy and small kindnesses to your responses.

August in a FIVE Personal Year Cycle

Together with the intended progress of your Five PYC, August asks that you slow down your pace and do some serious thinking. The practical, economic and basics of life beckon. Get down to bedrock and move up close and personal with the real everyday stuff that keeps the motor running. If you have not yet laid a good foundation for future growth and attainment, then now is a good time to do it. Take a good look at where you are in life. Is it where you want to be or are you doing far more simply because you feel you must? Are you moving forward in your strides or are you merely circling? Make a conscious effort to take care of what is seeking your attention. Doing this now will clear the way for more personal freedom in the months ahead. Being realistic now will open up a more direct path towards achieving your goals and expectations. Yes, much is expected from you, and it may not necessarily be in situations you yourself created. Yet, you must do your part to help and support as best you can.

Do not allow your sense of restlessness to scatter your resources, nor your chances for improvement and achievement. Perhaps you are not inclined towards the practical side of life, preferring to be out and about and prospecting for work, organising others to do it, rather than actually doing it. August however, asks that you catch up on what has been overlooked. Healthwise, listen to what your body is telling you. Meet all obstacles and challenges with determination and inspiration, always with the goal in view. With your happiness hormones sitting in challenge position, at times effort will be needed to maintain optimism and a sense of joy. August asks you to make necessary changes to the build – whether a career, a friendship, a home, a life.

Your best responses for August
- Much is expected from you, give only of your best.
- The necessities of life must be addressed, your support is needed.
- Be practical, organised and methodical in your approach.
- Be grounded, for yourself and others.
- Join in the celebrations and connections.

September in a FIVE Personal Year Cycle

September brings the high point or climax to the year. The vitality and energy that you feel this month will be difficult to ignore. You can almost feel a sense of freedom, of abandon even, which excites the senses and stirs your passion for progress, change and advancement. This is a busy time, but a time which also offers opportunity through people contact and interaction with the public. Do not shy away from associating and communicating with others, even those you do not know. It is an excellent time for you to be up and doing things. It's not a time to be idle, even for a moment. There are places to go and people to meet. This is an action month, a doing month, which includes lending a hand in support of others.

September is a good time for advertising your wares. If you want to publicise what you do, if you want others to know what you're selling, now's the time. Be aware, though, that there is a degree of uncertainty running through the month so do not throw caution to the winds. Acting in ways that are not you, being quick off the mark with your responses without thinking them through, will not win for you. There may be times when you feel like you're at a standstill, doing but not sure what. Feeling as though it's not you calling the shots, that you have little or no control. For sure, you will need to ground yourself if you are to grasp the changes and turn them into something positive. Take a trip somewhere with someone you care about. If that's out of the question then a nice easy drive perhaps. Avoid getting bored, do something different or maybe go out and buy something new or treat yourself to a spa or facial, a new outfit perhaps. A Maserati? Well, that depends on your bank balance ...

Your best responses for September
- Blend your needs with your wants.
- Look for opportunities to showcase your character, your people skills perhaps and more.
- Mingle, socialise, say 'yes' more.
- Listen to your spirit self.
- Be determined to make some good changes in your life.

October in a FIVE Personal Year Cycle

Family matters this month and October presents both sides of the equation – the beautiful side of family and the heavier side. However, it's the lighter side that Life wants you to experience, so set your focus on that. Enjoy family gatherings and outings, accepting invitations and giving them, include family you haven't seen for a while. Avoid leaning more towards family's heavier aspects – the duties and obligations, feeling that you're giving too much of yourself. Do what you can without feeling too much is expected. Pull back if you must, and rest a while. Home and family feature, and taking care of loved ones and meeting your commitments cannot be overlooked. The wonderful feeling that comes with helping and caring for others can be immeasurable. But in all this remember to take care of your own health and wellbeing. While it's impossible to ignore the tugging of what you feel you must do, even though you'd prefer it wasn't so, you will be delighted with the little successes and little praises you receive. For sure, going the extra mile in the workplace and in whatever situation you find yourself will bring dividends.

Your emotions can be taxed this month, so make a conscious effort to stay on top of things. Avoid feeling scattered, set boundaries and be organised. Deal with whatever comes your way by blending feelings with reason. Be aware, as your generosity, including your bank balance, may be stretched if you do not set limits. Avoid being insistent or persistent about what you 'know' to be for the best, especially for those closest to you. While giving advice is intended to help, it's also important to encourage others to make their own decisions. If it's not yours, let it go. October encourages you to care and support others while maintaining an appropriate distance and not stepping into over-care.

Your best responses for October
- Enjoy the great stuff about family and community, be a part of it.
- Remember that Life compels you to love them, but liking them is your choice.
- Do and give only what you can.
- Appreciate the success and progress, whether a little or a lot.
- Give more compliments, genuine ones, and you'll get more smiles and gratitude.

November in a FIVE Personal Year Cycle

November can be a busy time as preparations get under way for the Christmas period and the wind-down begins in anticipation for the holiday season. Perhaps you are not quite certain where or with whom you will be spending your Christmas. There is no need to concern yourself with these matters now. There will be time enough for that later. There's an introspective energy governing the month which one can feel, at times making it difficult to simply be happy without good reason. With joy and happiness sitting in challenge position, it's all the more reason why you need to make an effort to lighten things up in some well-intentioned way. Do something deliberately for the joy it brings. Call a friend, meet up with someone who makes you laugh more. It's a good time for a holiday, away from the everyday stuff of life. If that's not possible, maybe you can factor in just a few days away.

The month calls for thought and reflection. It is a time for you to look deep within yourself and come up with options in finding solutions to problems and situations that have been hampering you. Refuse to give into feelings of resentment, ultra-sensitivity or emotional upset if others do not understand you or what you are feeling. Living in the present moment without the regrets of yesterday and without the apprehension of what tomorrow may bring is the best gift you can give yourself. The month encourages spending time with special others in your life and for more quiet pursuits. Yet it also carries an undeniable busyness. Making time for 'you' is not an indulgence this month but a necessity, and your health will benefit from this. November challenges you to find joy and inspiration in *all* that life brings.

Your best responses for November
- Make time to be with your thoughts and those who want the best for you.
- Avoid giving into low moods.
- Go deeper in search of Life's meaning.
- Do what you do extra well.
- Do something that makes you happy.

December in a FIVE Personal Year Cycle

You will feel a sense of 'having it all together' as the month gets underway. A feeling that you are more in control, as you shift into top gear to meet all the demands and expectations of the holiday season. Good management will be needed, as your Five PYC puts your strength and ability to bounce back to the test. Take care of your health and avoid doing more than you can handle, even if you feel that you could take on the world. Be as one who sees all and helps to maintain balance. Put your executive skills to good use, encourage more and dictate less. While money may not be a concern for you at this time, make it your business to assess your financial position to avoid any shortfalls in the months ahead. In other words, don't just think you know where you stand, know where you stand.

All in all, this promises to be a good month with people coming and going as is expected during the festive season. Balance the material with the spiritual and you will find little to worry about. Be aware of that sensitivity during December, as people can be heard to say the wrong thing. Understand that words are just that and refuse to allow these feelings to dampen the enjoyment and festive mood. This is a busy time, and includes time spent with family, friends and others. A holiday away from home may be on the cards, or perhaps celebrations away from home, even if you had not previously planned for this. Your good judgement will be an asset in aiding you to achieve your plans. December encourages you to take charge without losing your sensitivity to the needs of others or to your own needs and feelings.

Your best responses for December
- Your mind has charge over your emotions, make this work for you.
- Balance work with leisure time.
- Make it your intention to bring people together in peace and harmony.
- If it's not important, let it go.
- Be confident in yourself and sensitive to others' vulnerabilities.

Six
Personal Year Cycle

The SIX Personal Year Cycle brings experiences intended to hone and polish the following qualities and areas of life –

Humanitarian Influence, Service, Home and Family, Relationships, Idealism, Charity, Truth and Justice, Artistic Influence, Harmony, Responsibility, Community, Generosity.

Its mandate is to prompt, encourage and at times push you to live these qualities to the very best of your ability in positive mode, and in so doing promote and sustain a constant state of evolving and becoming the whole and truly unique person you were born to be.

The SIX Personal Year Cycle

The Six PYC opens the second part of your present nine-year cycle. This is the year that will start to show the rewards of the work and application of your past efforts, of the past five years. Enjoy the success that it brings; you deserve it. Results will be evidenced in degrees, dependent on your responses and fulfilment to Life's expectations, demands and opportunities through previous Personal Year Cycles. This is your year for service and duty, which will be intermingled with pleasure as well as with challenges. It's important to note that, more than ever, your biggest gains, successes and progress come through what you do for others this year. Remember this when others test your patience and generosity.

The six being the number of ideals means that living according to what you consider right takes precedence. Be aware, though, that what you deem to be right, to be just, might not be the way someone else will see it. Be open to the fact that others also have the right to live according to their standards, so give them their space, even if you disagree with them. Bear in mind that acceptance and compromise do not mean that you are necessarily in accord with the situation or issue in question, nor do they mean that injustices become just. Rather, that you respect the other person's right to his or her say. Sometimes to agree to disagree is not only the best solution, in some cases it's the only solution. This year, your Six PYC asks you to be the teacher, the parent, the carer, the idealist, the creative, the lover. The best way is to lead by example. Give advice but leave the decisions up to them. Be there to support, to lend a hand, without adding the 'I told you so' when they stumble.

You will feel a degree of urgency with the wish to settle down, to be where you want to be, to settle affairs, both in business and in your private life. There's a feeling of wanting to wrap things up, so to speak. You want to have all the loose ends tied up so you can simply enjoy your life with those who matter, with those who hold a little piece of your heart. Appreciation and the addition of beauty and aesthetic qualities in and around the home will also be felt. With so much wanting your attention, keep in mind that this is not a time to rush things through. Some matters might need to be discussed and negotiated, so seek professional advice when necessary. Personal or business relationships will demand that you lend a hand and show that you care. Health is another area that features this year, yours or someone else's. Be sure to take care and not neglect it. The care and humanitarian element is a major part of this year's energy and cannot be dismissed. You can expect that family, including the extended family, children, parents and relatives, will feature more in your life this year. It's a year which leans towards romance, relationship commitments and marriage. When love is true it gives intimate relationships the opportunity to progress to the next level. On the downside, love that is not true can lead to separations and arguments. Be more focused on the important stuff. Be aware of the state of your love relationship and ask yourself the all-important questions. Are you attentive to your partner's needs? Do you make time for romance or do you consider life is way too busy for that? Do you share home responsibilities? What about the children? For sure, your time can be taken up looking after others' needs outside the home, but in all this it pays to remember that you and those closest to you matter most and need your love and attention first and foremost. Enjoy the family celebrations, weddings, family get-togethers and festivities that the year brings. Take time to enjoy the beauty of Life and be grateful for the blessings.

Your best responses in a SIX Personal Year Cycle
- Be attentive and do not fall for false praise.
- Be supportive of those in need, including yourself.
- Make time for your health.
- Be prepared to care for the wellbeing of another.
- Enjoy the success.

- Make time for the beautiful side of family.
- Give lots of compliments and praise, and far less criticism.
- Bring loved ones together to celebrate.
- Be grateful for your family and your part in it.
- Judge less, romance more.

January in a SIX Personal Year Cycle

In this year of duties and responsibilities, January starts off with a rather introspective energy. There's something which does not allow you the full freedom to be or do as you would like. Perhaps your health is not up to par and you cannot scoot around as fast as usual. The subjective feel in January's numbers, however, does not mean you take to your corner. It means the best way to carry out your intentions is to go more with what your Six PYC brings you this month, adding flexibility to enable you to make changes and adjustments so you can keep moving along at a comfortable pace. When you are prepared to do this, you also allow that element of luck scripted into this month's offerings room to move and become real. Considering the activity and fun of the holiday season continuing into January, your preference may be to get away. A vacation, or even a few days away, sounds pretty good. Yet you may find that even in the midst of the busyness, your leanings are more towards doing something special, something different, instead of the usual or the ordinary and mundane.

Calm your mind if it goes into overdrive in view of recent challenges. Make time for what is important to you and what brings you joy. Trust that what is not to your liking will work itself out in time. For sure, you may be surprised at how things will take a turn for the better. Join in with community activities and enjoy the social aspect, the lighter side of life, which often runs parallel to any annoyances. Get in touch with your inner strength and feel comfortable with it. This month you may find that the important breakthrough or change will come about

123

by way of your thoughts more so than your actions. January challenges you to trust in something beyond the ordinary and to look beyond what's directly visible for answers and solutions.

Your best responses for January
- Make time for something special this month.
- Spend time with like-minded friends.
- If Life is pulling you back, don't question it, release the controls and enjoy the scenery.
- Avoid being critical of others, even if you feel let down.
- Get in tune with Life and move in time to Her music.

February in a SIX Personal Year Cycle

As you move into February you will notice that you have more control over your emotions. For sure, there is much to do and you will need to exert sound management if you are to take your intentions where they can best serve you and others. Matters regarding the family home and/or business improvement will surface, with any decisions needing to be weighed and balanced. When viewing your options, use good judgement in your choices before enacting your decisions. It might not be anything major, but do take your time and get it right. Always aim for the best possible outcome. While family matters are there for you, do not allow yourself to get bogged down or overwhelmed with all that you want to do. This frame of mind will only hinder you from taking small and necessary steps towards what is important to you.

A level-headed and logical approach towards details involving money matters is needed throughout February. Do not be alarmed if you experience difficulty in dealing with those matters that call for your attention. The wonderful thing is that others are willing to help you out, so be gracious in acceptance. Though money is there for you, it is not a time for spending at leisure, nor for indulging in unnecessary purchases. The year will bring expenses as it progresses, granted. But it will also bring its fair share of reward and success to balance. It is not all work and no play. There is the possibility of a trip here, which may mix business with pleasure. February challenges you to bring more organisation and structure into your life. Not in a way that adds more work, but in a way that frees you up from it. Meet your obligations but do not make them masters over your happiness and good intentions.

Your best responses for February
- Life will test you for strength, resilience, authority and stamina.
- Be methodical and decisive in all you do. As the saying goes, 'the buck stops with you' this month.
- There's importance in getting things right, not so in rushing things through.
- Sometimes you just have to say, 'Not today'.
- Be more business-minded.

March in a SIX Personal Year Cycle

March is geared towards finalities, with a degree of closure on some matter. This may be in your mind, if not in actuality. Sometimes it can be a conclusion to something you've been working to complete, and can bring a feeling of release with it, a feeling that the project is finally finished and you'll be able to move on to something new. Emotions run deep throughout this month as life tests your optimism in view of better things to come. Sensing a business opportunity? You will need to get past these testing feelings and clear your mind for a better and more realistic perspective if you are to take advantage of it. There will be much for you to do with others – family, friends and business associates. Express your emotions constructively and phrase your words for successful communication. Remember that people cannot look inside your heart, that it's necessary to vocalise your feelings in ways that are positive and honest in expression. This way you give those in your circle the opportunity to respond in ways that are supportive and progressive.

Creative endeavour is present, and also opportunity for broadening your vista. Success is on the cards, there's no need for you to push for it. It's a time for taking your talents and kindness to the world, not for locking them up. Attend to any matters calling for closure with empathy and sensitivity. Deal with matters of the past while you look ahead to what possibilities await you in the future. While you might get pulled into life's drama, avoid being dramatic. Demonstrate compassion and understanding in your dealings with others, and of course when dealing with yourself. Stay clear of narrow-minded people who may tempt you to respond from a tunnel-vision perspective. Dare to be broad-minded and inclusive. March challenges you to express love, friendship and joy in the midst of responsibility, duty, conclusions and sensitivity.

Your best responses for March
- Do not allow hurts to dim your light – shine brighter.
- Let go of the past with love.
- Spend more time with friends than acquaintances.
- Good communication can bring you down a notch or take you up.
- Allow your feelings and emotions positive expression.

April in a SIX Personal Year Cycle

April brings change. It does not have to be anything remarkable or ground-breaking. Perhaps it's a different way of approaching a problem, or something that has resurfaced. Be sure to make use of your talents this month, especially your intellectually creative ones. Clear away the clutter from your mind and get those thoughts and ideas churning. You may not want to, but do deal with the situation which has presented itself using the courage on offer. Turn on those little grey cells and encourage them to come up with the best solutions. Be proactive and plan for what you want, but at the same time do not close yourself off by leaning into single-mindedness. Tune in to what is going on around you; in this way you will be able to take on board what is beneficial and leave the rest behind. Don't lose confidence if something feels overwhelming, or if someone does not see the options and possibilities that you see. This can be a sensitive period, but only if you allow yourself to falsely believe you are less than capable of dealing with what you must.

You can get caught up in the hectic pace of the month as it moves you towards new opportunities through its challenges. Maybe it is difficult for you to fully grasp what's possible or what you want to do, what you can do. April's energy is charged with a go-get-it, assertive attitude and challenged by a hesitant and indecisive sensitivity. Be aware of this and do not be put off by the abstract. Put your skills to good use and fine-tune what you have conceived so far. Check the details, look behind the obvious, it's often the place where answers rest. Collect your information and materials in preparation. The months ahead will allow your plans and ideas to form and shape themselves, give them time to materialise, give what is other than the best time to resolve itself. No rush needed.

Your best responses for April
- Blend assertiveness with sensitivity, soften your authority without weakening your position.
- Avoid taking negative input personally.
- Take charge in ways that don't alienate others.
- Give yourself space to think.
- Have the courage and initiative to enact the ideas that hold merit.

May in a SIX Personal Year Cycle

Your relationships with others, people connections and how genuine or not they are, will push you to make decisions which you may be reluctant to make. It is easy to maintain good standing with others when everything is going well. Difficulties arise, however, when those who are a part of your life oppose that which you consider to be positive and beneficial. Sometimes it doesn't matter how much you do for others, nor how caring and kind you are towards them. Sometimes relationships, no matter how close or distant, need to be trimmed or severely pruned in order to establish a new and more genuine base. It is also possible that Life may deem a disconnection, even if you wish it wasn't so. Do try to see things in perspective as you attend to details and the things that concern you. Be kind to yourself as your sensitivity may be bruised this month.

There will be someone in your circle to test your peacemaking qualities during May. Something surfaces which you may feel is out of your control to fix or make better. You can avoid upsetting yourself unduly by allowing those concerned to have their say and make their own decisions, even if you do not agree with them. Remember that respecting another's opinion does not mean that you approve or agree with them. What it means is that you are spiritually and intellectually conscious enough to respect the right of others to make their own choices. Should you decide to end a relationship, business or personal, be certain to do so using tact, diplomacy and empathy. Why, you may ask. Because your Six PYC demands this approach from you to ensure that you come out a winner. Do not mistake these requirements; be assertive and stand your ground, but always without making the other person feel less of a human being.

Your best responses for May
- Know when to play your assertiveness card and when to play your cooperative card.
- Accept the chance to truly shine, to rise above the heaviness around you.
- Take charge of what presents itself with courage and sensitivity.
- Avoid overstepping your authority, accept what is deemed to be.
- If it's not yours to carry, release it with gratitude.

June in a SIX Personal Year Cycle

You will welcome the positive feelings as you head into June, a light energy you wish could last forever. You can afford to be a little selfish now by doing something for yourself, even if it's a leisurely walk in nature, amongst its greenery or its waterways. There are times when we all need a little nurturing, and whether it's chicken soup, or lunch out with good friends with whom you can laugh and feel the child within you come alive, you have June's blessing. Go for it! The month is ideal for a holiday, a time to socialise and to enjoy good times with those special people in your life, the young and not so young. But in all this there's a creative energy which subtly encourages you to envision something solid and purposeful for your dreams and imaginings, for your plans. Self-expression takes a forward step, but it's up to you to make sure that how you showcase your talents, ability and character this month takes you forward and not backward. There are business opportunities and money making ventures to be checked out. Make the most of it! Consider any good advice for improvement and advancement.

Emotions, feelings and the way you communicate these are at an all-time high, so take care to steer them in a positive direction. Something may trigger sadness – if this happens, feel it and release it with love. You may not like some of the things you hear, or how some people do things, but restrain yourself from criticising. Your ideals and aspirations are at a high point, don't dampen them, spread them around so that others may also benefit. Be a person of vision, envisioning how you can share joy, inspiration and success by the way you respond to Life's offerings.

Your best responses for June
- With an all-or-nothing element running through June, make your choices count. Do something substantial.
- Be the friend you want others to be. Inspire and be inspired!
- Nurture your dreams – they are the beginnings of what can be.
- Do something for the sheer joy it brings you.
- Showcase your creative and artistic side.

July in a SIX Personal Year Cycle

Get yourself into gear this month as it's the practical and realistic matters your Six PYC will expect you to make a priority. Good economic planning is essential as accounts step up and ask to be settled. It's a month which may require a tightening of your wallet rather than an open wallet, especially if you over indulged your spending last month. There are issues and tasks to be talked over or taken care of, some connected to family, some to work or community. This does not mean that you need to be on call at all times – however, if there is a genuine request for help, or simply lending a hand, then July says give it willingly. System, order and good management are essential if you are to accomplish anything worthwhile. There are lessons to be learned here and progress to be made, so be on the lookout for those with experience to help you out if necessary. Dig in, do your work, showcase your caring side and it will be appreciated and rewarded. There is the possibility that you could be working away from home or that your work or home base is different from the usual.

When you step in line with July's strong work ethic, it offers much in the way of accomplishment. Rest, however, must also be factored in if you are to maintain a healthy balance. For sure, you may feel that you have little control over certain matters, but it's important to the success of the month that you avoid feeling boxed in or overwhelmed. When feeling like this, it's a sure sign that you have overstepped what your PYC expected from you, that you are doing way too much. Pull back a little. Take care of your health and attend any medical checks. Most importantly, be sure to slot in fun times with those you love. Blend work with social outings – it's the perfect balance.

Your best responses for July
- Take the chance to take something further into the building stage.
- Pull back somewhat if commitments feel heavy.
- Pencil in a 'to do' list to take advantage of July's serious work ethic.
- Balance work with social relaxation.
- Be more like the tortoise than the hare.

August in a SIX Personal Year Cycle

August allows you a little more freedom from responsibilities, it does not intend you to be work-bound. There is a sense of excitement and activity – allow yourself to feel it. Change is in the air and perhaps you are planning a change or two yourself. Now's the time! Look at where you are and where you want to go and make any adjustments you consider would bring you closer to achieving that. In all this, there's also the chance that Life may Herself bring change. Remember you cannot return this to Sender if you do not like it or want it. But it is within your power to strategise the best response possible for what you do want. August promises to be a forward-moving month, and fast-paced at that. It offers progress, improvement and opportunity when you make your attitude both adaptable and flexible. Yes, there is a difference between the two, and while flexibility is on offer, adaptability sits in challenge position, and it will challenge you to be it at its best. Hence the need for marrying the two. Expect to make new contacts as well as connecting with some you have not seen for a while.

Your interest will be sparked as you see an opportunity for future success – consider it. Travel is an option, if not to foreign places then certainly getting out and about within nearer boundaries, even just moving around more locally. There is an air of uncertainty as the unexpected is likely to surface, so be prepared for a surprise or two. Minimise risks with any business dealings by doing your homework on all aspects of the venture or proposal. Read the small print. Avoid being overly sensitive to criticism and restrain yourself from overreacting. Though the month offers you more personal freedom, it also comes with personal responsibility. Keep a check on any health issues and enjoy the buzz and people contact on offer.

Your best responses for August
- Make the changes you want to see.
- Not a time to be alone – mix and mingle, be sociable.
- You may feel like bending some rules – just don't break them.
- Be flexible to what Life brings, be as the willow – free-moving and unbreakable.
- Be aware of and consider any opportunities on offer.

September in a SIX Personal Year Cycle

It's wonderful to be rewarded for all the effort, work and discipline you put into your intentions, into your goals. September brings this home to you. Enjoy the success, Life's pat on the back that says 'You deserve this. Well done!' Though responsibilities and commitments are heightened at this time, you will, however, come to the realisation and satisfaction that you are getting somewhere and be pleased with your progress and accomplishment. Your caring and loving side may be given a bit of a workout, but refuse to dwell on any negativity. For sure, someone close to you may test your reserves. You may be prompted to give back the same way, but that would only take you backward. Express your feelings, your emotions, more constructively, with dignity and grace, without giving in to idle gossip or stooping to a level that is less than the best of you.

With the demands made upon you during September, it would be easy for you to lean towards an attitude of detachment, to close your heart even, to the care, service and generosity which your Six PYC demands of you. If you are not in accord with what others are saying or doing, remember that understanding and empathy will steer you towards a resolution. Give those in your life the chance to make their own decisions and to voice their point of view. Give your advice and accept their response. Don't push it. If it's not yours to own, let it be. Choose to see those in your life with love first. Matters connected to

131

family, relationships, marriage, children and other things connected here will feature this month. Look for what is good in them. Look for the goodness and kindness in yourself and let that be your calling card. September challenges you to express joy and inspiration while administering service and care to others. Make time for someone special, someone who makes you laugh. Enjoy the celebrations and be happy with all you have accomplished thus far.

Your best responses for September
- Give more compliments, period.
- Take care of any illness, yours or someone else's.
- Listen more, talk less.
- Enjoy the beauty of your surroundings – feel it.
- Cook, bake, invite, visit, and share generously.

October in a SIX Personal Year Cycle

October brings a desire for 'time out' in the midst of your busy Six PYC. It may prove difficult to attain peace of mind, simply because there is so much to do and so much going on around you. And yet, this is the very reason for making time for just that – to quiet your mind. In turn this will help to re energise and restore your strength and inner reserves. You will find yourself doing a great deal of thinking as you assess your situation and how to consequently offload some of life's demands. Perhaps some of these thoughts may be of a secretive nature; things that you do not wish to discuss with others, or even want others to know about. And that's OK.

Sometimes the mind can magnify the negative in our lives to a degree where we become consumed by matters that are out of our control. Be aware and avoid overwhelming your mental state with too much thought. Tap into your reservoir of wisdom and believe that in the macro of life all is well. Be kind to yourself and do not allow anxiety or apprehension to take hold. Your Six PYC is asking you to rise above the ordinary, to see and do with more wisdom than muscle, with more 'knowing' than hard convincing. The freedom to fully move and do is in challenge position this month, so be creative. October asks you to pull back, to not waste your energy pushing for what you want, to instead let it come to you. The more you release the controls, the more control you'll have. There's an element of luck running through the month so send in those coupons. Relax more, stress less and let the luck scripted for this time free access, free entry. Say 'yes' only to what you love and 'maybe' or 'no' to the rest.

Your best responses for October
- Observe more.
- Listen with your soul.
- Ask the big questions and go within for the answers.
- Trust in Life's process of working things out.
- Spend time with someone who understands you.

November in a SIX Personal Year Cycle

November moves you away from emotional overload and more into the intellectual and practical arena. In other words, Life is telling you that your best responses are the ones based on a more logical and reasoning brain rather than an emotional one. This of course applies as much to emotional situations and experiences as it does to business decisions or practical matters. In this way you are better able to maintain clarity and a more realistic perspective for yourself and those in your care. It's a busy month with people to meet and much to plough through, so put on your business-minded attitude and get moving. There will be matters to attend to in relation to work and property, yours or that of someone you know. This can be anything from repairing something, to renovating, refurbishing, or buying and selling. Life will expect you to stay on board and not take to your corner other than for rest periods. It's a time which brings experiences intent on giving your strength, resilience and business acumen a workout.

Previous plans regarding property may call for a re-arrangement or a re-evaluation, of looking for improvement. This month, tackle all dealings with good management, efficiency and resourcefulness. Being mentally alert will win for you. Avoid rushing things through or becoming overly anxious about your expectations and what you think you should be doing. Family matters may tug at your heartstrings, do what you can. Support others without carrying their 'load' for them. A time when matter meets Spirit. Harmonise both for the best possible outcome. Find a balance in your relationships that helps promote harmony. Mix with influential people and accept their help if it is offered; this is not a time for you to be coy. Life brings reward and recognition for your efforts, character and your service to others. Monetary gain may also be imminent.

Your best responses for November
- Attend to any health matters.
- Make time for rest and recreation.
- You may want to do more, but you cannot do the impossible.
- Family matters are in focus, be gracious in your responses.
- Celebrate family and being a part of it.

December in a SIX Personal Year Cycle

The month of December brings a climax or a sense of release to much that has been happening in your life. You will be pleased with the conclusions and the coming together of certain aspects of your dealings and relationships. At the same time, the emotionally charged energy which the month carries may activate some deep emotional feelings. Do not be surprised to catch yourself out looking back at the events which shaped your year, which we often do at this time. Your mind might take you on a tour down memory lane. A little like what happens when we go through photos and sentimental memorabilia when moving house or when clearing stuff. It's not unusual for this to stir up a mix of emotions. If this happens, be sure to allow these emotions the freedom of expression, rather than denying them or suppressing them. Understand that life is a mix of disappointments as well as successes. Remember this and accept that certain things have been unavoidable or out of your hands. Remind yourself also that you did your best. And in this equation, for sure your love and good intentions count far more than anything else.

With change factored in for December, this could mean that circumstances may be somewhat different this Christmas season. But in all this remain optimistic, as things may be more positive than you had perhaps expected. There are social gatherings and celebrations on offer, so join in and enjoy the food as much as the company. There is a great deal of love around you, allow yourself to feel its energy and give back in kind. Be gracious, celebrate and share the joy and good wishes amidst friends and family. December challenges you to relish the love and appreciation and to actively participate in the spirit of giving and receiving.

Your best responses for December
- Do something that activates your happiness hormones.
- Keep good friends close by.
- Say 'yes' more when you are invited to social outings.
- Let go of what has reached completion, with love.
- Celebrate Life, *all* of it – the sad, the glad, the annoying, the tranquil, the ugly, the beautiful … as it endeavours to shape you into the *all* of who you were born to be.

Seven
Personal Year Cycle

The SEVEN Personal Year Cycle brings experiences intended to hone and polish the following qualities and areas of life –

Deliberate Thought, Perfection, Specialisation, Meditation, Intelligence, Trust in a Higher Power, Skill, Intuition, Science, Other Worldly Things, Dignity, Solitude.

Its mandate is to prompt, encourage and at times push you to live these qualities to the very best of your ability in positive mode, and in so doing promote and sustain a constant state of evolving and becoming the whole and truly unique person you were born to be.

The SEVEN Personal Year Cycle

After the busy pace and responsibilities of last year, your Seven PYC may hint at being more laid back, but it will still have much for you to do. Call this a sabbatical, a retreat, or a vacation year. Whatever term you use to describe it really does not matter. What matters is that you get to know all that it encourages, expects and demands from you, and be willing to align yourself to its requirements. Of the nine Personal Year Cycles, three of them bring significant changes – this is one of them, along with the One and Nine PYCs. New ways of thinking and acting are a part of this year's energy. There's also a lowering of physical energy and for this reason you need to pay attention to your health. Make health a priority this year. Avoid overdoing – mentally, emotionally or physically. Rest up and make healthy eating a priority. Watch out for low moods, get help if you need it. Feelings of aloneness, 'the blues', and a pulling away from the social scene will be stronger than usual, even in the midst of many activities. Others may misunderstand your need to withdraw into your own space, to spend more time with your thoughts, in quiet contemplation. The year offers experiences and opportunities to encourage more meetings with your higher self and that realm of wisdom and inner knowing.

You will come to realise the importance of spirituality in your life and the necessity to balance it with the material. Allow for this, as it will recharge your body and mind as well as your spirit. Questions will arise, big questions, and will push you to search for answers. This is Life inviting you into a higher plane of conscious awareness. This year is intended to expand your knowledge, skill and development into areas that are not of the material world, and yet they influence the material world, immensely. The Seven PYC is not one for you to go after what you want, nor to start new ventures. It's a year for receiving what comes to you. It's not about doing nothing. But it's definitely not for chasing material success. For sure, accept opportunities that come your way, but understand that this is not a time for you to push for, or to demand what you want. It's OK to slow down when you do not feel up to par. Stepping back and going with the flow will win for you this year. Step into Life and walk with Her. Do not waste your time trying to convince others to see things your way. They're not listening and doing so will only cause you distress and bring further delays.

A change with the possibility of a loss or break-up of old interests or situations offers a new perspective, a new way of seeing things. When this is understood and accepted, stress and confusion will lose their intensity, problems will be resolved and the luck of the number seven will invite itself in. In all this, though, it is not a time for you to gamble your life savings or to take risks. Your Seven PYC is asking you to rise above the heaviness which binds – from emotional reaction, from resentment, envy, or feelings of lack. This year, Life asks you to respond from a higher level – the level of wisdom. For best results let your wisdom rule over your emotions and intellect. It's a year geared towards intellectual interests, a new study or anything related to advancing your knowledge or taking a skill to another level. It's time to raise the bar! Indulge in therapies that calm and soothe you. The time is right for travel connected to learning. If you have been thinking of a trip away to further your training, knowledge or cultural interests, or to spend time with special others, now is the time. This is no ordinary year. It's one which asks you to accept and enjoy the differences, rather than wanting to make them similar. It's a year for choosing who you want in your life. Spend time with the select few rather than anybody and everybody. Make the most of this soul development year – it's special.

Your best responses in a SEVEN Personal Year Cycle
- Choose a talent or ability and skill it to the max.
- Take time to rest and care for your health.
- Enjoy your own company, simply be.
- Choose your friends intentionally, not haphazardly.
- Let things come to you.
- Observe more, talk less.
- Celebrate the different, the unusual.
- Resist chasing after what you want.
- Do not let your moods take a dive.
- Trust that all is well in the big picture, even if you cannot see it.

January in a SEVEN Personal Year Cycle

The year is set to start with a sense of confidence and commitment. You will be eager to be up and doing. Keep in mind, however, that your Seven PYC requires you to take a walk on the spiritual side, as experiences and situations come up to test your inner strength and resilience to life's challenges. This is not a month for you to hide from the world. Showcase your talents, your creations and see what comes from this, what Life brings. As it is for a boxer, experiences will be there to test whether your ability to get up after a knockdown is real or pretend. Whether it's a skinned knee or something else you're nurturing, Life will expect you to get back in the ring and continue living and giving nothing less than your best. It's the only way you can expect the outcome to your responses to be the best possible.

Without a doubt you will be kept busy throughout January with issues related to property, business or family matters. You will be expected to be the manager, the one who takes care of others and to work things out with astute business efficiency to ensure a successful outcome. Expect to make decisions and to meet commitments and obligations as you offload responsibilities connected to the past. Do not allow your emotions to take over now, but rather, be detached and maintain a clear and focused mind. Some of the issues that surface may be connected to family matters and it is in this respect that your emotions may want to override your clear thinking. Life offers you the opportunity to leave much of the responsibility behind you and to move forward with the promise of new ideas and possibilities. Avoid becoming bogged down with money issues. By all means, balance your books if you need to. Have faith and keep in mind that situations are working themselves out even if you cannot see this at present.

Your best responses for January
- Assume authority but avoid force.
- Take care of any health matters.
- Mix with others but avoid becoming them.
- Give your advice softly.
- Show genuine appreciation.

February in a SEVEN Personal Year Cycle

This month brings conclusions and a degree of finality to certain issues. Some of these finalities you yourself choose, others Life chooses for you. Whether it's what you expected, what you wanted or didn't want, accept it for what it is, nothing more. Know that without first accepting a change we cannot begin to consider our response. Take a step back now and reflect on the situation before turning the steering wheel, before moving in any direction. February carries an energy of deep feeling challenged by strong intentions. Going in too deeply can create mental confusion and feelings of aloneness, so don't let yourself go there. Deliberately choose to leave behind anything that has been holding you back. Remind yourself of your strength and wisdom to move in the best direction, when you are ready. February brings you rewards from past efforts – love that!

A situation or someone can stir an impulse to argue or criticise – resist! Your sense of freedom, of being able to move and do at your own pace, may be somewhat thwarted throughout February. Look at what's open to you and make any changes that allow you more independence. Now's the time to let go of what is no longer beneficial to your growth, to your advancement, in character and business. Release it with love and don't look back. Do this also with people who don't have good intentions for you, create a healthy space between you and them. In all this, your Seven PYC asks that you demonstrate love and empathy. Maintain your focus on Life's beauty and magnificence, above all else. Express your feelings with more joy and deliberately move towards all things positive. Invite others into your space, those who want what is good for you. Socialise more and accept the help, love and success that is offered and given, share the good times and make beautiful memories.

Your best responses for February
- Be that kind of person you want others to be.
- Make the change if it's for betterment.
- Let go of what *is* no longer.
- Feel the love, accept it and share it.
- Create something from your heart – a poem, a cake, a beautiful experience.

March in a SEVEN Personal Year Cycle

March in your Seven PYC opens with the chance for you to start a fresh page. It encourages you to take a step up to higher ground so you can get a clearer look at all that's on offer. You may feel that Life is pushing you to be self-supportive, self-sufficient – and you're right, It is. You're in charge this month, so get the feel of what it's like to take the lead and do it. Step into it. Life is encouraging you, even pushing you, to come up with solutions, with new ways of doing things, new ideas, looking at the old with new eyes. It's exciting as well as scary, especially if you prefer to be part of a team rather than 'out there'. March's energy is for something new, yet this is challenged by the beckoning of all things practical, including family responsibilities and commitments.

This is not the time for going at hectic speed, but about laying the groundwork for what you want, however long that takes to get right. You may feel like you're putting in the effort but getting nowhere fast. So, stop and ground yourself. Bring in more structure and be more methodical in executing your plans. March encourages you to take charge and assume authority, first and foremost over yourself. Dare to implement the courage and foresight this month offers. Your Seven PYC is not about pushing for what you want but about aligning yourself with and making use of what comes to you. In all this though, you can still feel the impulse to do, to achieve, and that's OK. Understand that your Seven PYC is asking that you make plans, that you foresee a start. Be sure to enjoy the active pace of the month, immerse yourself in it, but if you feel like retreating for a while, do so, solely in your own company, or with a special other.

Your best responses for March
- Be gentle with your health
- Avoid aggression when your peace and harmony is disrupted; wisdom and understanding are the better options.
- Encourage, support and show others the way, but do not carry them.
- Use mental creativity more than grunt to achieve your purpose.
- Consider your ideas for practicality and workability.

April in a SEVEN Personal Year Cycle

You will find yourself very busy this month as you step up to meet Life's opportunities, demands and expectations. April is people orientated, which is understandable given that the month brings relationships to centre stage. How you relate with whoever crosses your path has the capacity to incite joy or crisis and anything in between. Of course the focus is on those who share your life, whether at work or in your personal space. We have opposing energies at play during April. One has a take-charge, assertive attitude and the other has a let me be, 'make love not war' attitude. Hence, the more accurately you distinguish which of these is the better option in any given situation, the more successful and peaceful the outcome. Your Seven PYC says 'observe more". In view of this, observe the situation first and then decide if your best choice is to step up and take charge or to stay put and play your 'let it be' card. In addition, focus on a win-win outcome for all concerned. In all this, there's a chance that the other may not want to be a part of your life. Accept that there's a limit to what you can do. When your intention includes love and peace, then know that you have raised the bar to its highest point.

As you go about the business of living, you may find that your heart is not really in it. There's a reason for this. Your happiness hormones are in the too hard basket, and someone or some situation will surely put this to the test at some time this month. This does not mean that you have to be unhappy. It just means that the joy and fun side of you needs to be more deliberately encouraged. Dare to express joy and optimism regardless as you give any problems time to work themselves out. There is an underlying spiritual feel to the month, a chance to shine ever so brightly. Take it.

Your best responses for April
- Check details, the small stuff.
- Encourage peace and harmony.
- Don't be aggressive, nor allow yourself to be walked over.
- Blend patience and cooperation with assertiveness.
- Pay attention to what you communicate by how you communicate it.

May in a SEVEN Personal Year Cycle

There's a somewhat lighter feel as May's energy begins to take effect. It's a time when Life decrees less hard work and responsibility and more enjoyment. There's an impulse for leisurely spending here so be aware of this before you hit the shops. Include others, invite friends to join you as you engage more socially this month. It's a time to nurture and appreciate friends. Be the friend you want others to be. Communication is key and the impulse to talk someone down may tempt you. Take care that the spontaneous energy you feel doesn't have you being less than gracious and causing upsets with those who share your life. There's a creative influence here, so make the most of it. Don't focus only on fun times. There are many ways to put your creativity to work, such as incubating dreams and ideas, or in more practical areas. Attend a talk or catch a movie that inspires you in some way. May also gives you the chance to be an inspiration to others by the way you live and respond to Life. Be that!

Take part in any creative or artistic genre that gives you joy and release from negative emotions. Dance, write, paint, bake, garden, or anything else that makes your heart sing. A holiday sounds good too! You may feel a distinct tug at your emotions as issues arise which you wish would just go away. Maintain your equilibrium and use your wisdom. Though May's energy is emotional and sensitive, your Seven PYC says wisdom is your best response. Be aware of feeling overly sensitive when you hear something you do not like. If things seem to be going at snail's pace, reassure yourself that beneath the surface all is progressing. May encourages you to express joy and optimism in all you do.

Your best responses for May
- Be understanding and helpful without getting involved.
- Meet all opposition with tact, diplomacy and good character.
- Enjoy getting together with friends – enjoy Life!
- Be sensitive to others' feelings, but it's not about walking on eggshells.
- Have fun, let your hair down, but do it with decorum.

June in a SEVEN Personal Year Cycle

June comes in with a more matter-of-fact, let's get the job done kind of energy. The great thing about it is that if you align yourself to June's work ethic you will get so much accomplished, without having to put in the extra effort required when you are working against your PYC requirements. You may not feel like doing this, and perhaps your inspiration and enthusiasm may be more on the low side. But you will certainly gain more freedom later if you can shift yourself into gear to do at least what is necessary, if nothing more. Sometimes we miss out on success because we're not ready. Good management of your affairs this month will ensure your preparedness for taking advantage of future opportunities. Avoid stressing over your present financial status if it's somewhat stretched or restricted. Things will improve in time. Attend to all papers and documents with a discriminating mind before signing.

Waiting for others to take care of matters won't work, so the sooner you gain control and get started the better you will feel. There's no need to create more work for yourself – don't look for new things to do, just attend to what is essential now. Give your health priority and take time to rest, there's a lot happening. If circumstances appear to be slowing you down, keep moving forward at your own pace. The domestic scene beckons with more serious stuff than fun stuff, all the more reason why you need to plan for the fun stuff. You cannot be expected to know everything, so do get help or advice from those who are more expert about such matters. The big bonus this month is that Life offers you the chance to take that dream or idea you've been working on to reality stage.

Your best responses for June
- Slow down, be patient, it will come together in its time.
- June is not a time for splurging on gifts, it's more for life's necessities.
- Get real with people and situations.
- Be there for others without putting yourself or your needs last.
- A chance to showcase your good character and standing. Gotta love that!

July in a SEVEN Personal Year Cycle

The month of July brings the promise of change and more personal freedom. It's not a time for sitting still for too long, but rather a time for immersing yourself in what's going on around you, and even further afield as circumstances allow. This month your Seven PYC encourages you to not settle for just anything. Search for what can be, for the good you want, the progress you want to see. It's an all or nothing energy that July carries – make it an all. Don't sit back, think of ways that will help to fulfil your plans. July encourages travel and movement. If your circumstances do not permit a trip abroad, then move around in your own backyard, in your own city. Take advantage of the people buzz this month. It's a great time to connect with others – for both social and business reasons. Consider what comes your way for workability and improvement. Change is in the air, even if it's simply rearranging the furniture or buying something new.

You may feel some discontent, a restlessness within you, one that can have you pushing others to see things your way. You do not suffer fools easily this month, but take care that you do not act foolishly and undo the good work you have so far accomplished. Help is available to you, but for your part you will need to be resourceful as well as interested. Be alert to any unexpected changes.

If they are not to your liking, give yourself time before responding, avoid hasty decisions. Take legal matters seriously and give them your undivided attention. July challenges you to move forward, in your mind, if nothing else. At the end of the month you will either have accomplished something worthwhile or next to nothing. It's that kind of a month. A month in which you will either move with Life or lag nonchalantly – you choose.

Your best responses for July
- Be resourceful, show initiative.
- Be attentive to the opportunities that come through others.
- Help others see their ability to succeed.
- Consider possible consequences before bending or breaking any rules.
- Feel July's energy and move with it – with excitement but not with irresponsibility.

August in a SEVEN Personal Year Cycle

As you move into this latter part of the year, momentum speeds up with much on the agenda. Family and all things connected to it will place much in the way of commitments and responsibilities squarely on your shoulders. You will be pleased, though, that it's not all about needs and obligations, for these are intermingled with pleasant social outings and celebrations. Enjoy the company and zest for life that children and young people involve you in. Help out with any problems where you can and give of yourself graciously. For sure, August is about supporting and helping those in your life, but it is not intended that you lose yourself in it and miss out on the beauty, love and romance that is also factored into this month's energy. This month is as much about beautiful and loving experiences as it is about responsibilities.

There will be times when you may feel somewhat restricted or even overwhelmed. Times when situations and relationships may feel more painful than joyful. Talking things over with someone who understands and making any necessary changes and adjustments will lighten the way you feel and make life less challenging. Treat yourself kindly and factor in adequate rest. This will avert the possibility of illness, which can be brought on by doing too much or from stressful situations. Your emotions supersede your intellect and responding with reason and a sense of authority may prove difficult. In all this, refuse to be stubborn and keep any low moods at a distance. If things seem to be going at a slower tempo than you would like, enjoy time out with your thoughts rather than adopting a forceful attitude. Enjoy the simple pleasures that August brings you in the midst of its responsibilities. Maintain your independence and individuality with grace and generosity.

Your best responses for August
- Be the one who cares, for others' wellbeing as well as your own.
- See the beauty around you, not just the needs.
- Showcase your love of family and humanity.
- Love will grow when it is given and received truthfully, from the heart.
- August brings appreciation and success – accept it with humility and gratitude.

September in a SEVEN Personal Year Cycle

You may find that any major activity will be a drag on your energy levels this month. The thought of escaping to the tranquillity of a desert island is something you could easily entertain. If you can manage a few days away from the usual, do so. It will be welcomed by your mind as much as your body. Make sure that whoever you invite to accompany you is someone who enjoys stillness as much as social activities. If time away is not possible then make time for quiet mental pursuits closer to home. There's an introspective energy through September that can lower your moods as well as your stamina. But you can manage both when you allow Life to unfold rather than pushing and prodding for It to reveal itself.

You may be aware of a sense of something different. It can almost feel as though you don't belong or fit in with what is going on around you. Feelings that others are not treating you with the respect and equality you deserve may also surface. Even if this is the case, refuse to be forceful – it won't work. This year Life is giving you experiences to showcase your wisdom, not your brute force. Pull back, give those in your circle the space they need to be themselves, both physically and mentally. Trust that things are working out even if progress is not visible. Step back and away from disagreements. Allow such things the necessary time to resolve themselves. Take care of your health, do more of what you love. Do more of what makes you happy. Be as one who sees the grand over the ordinary. This will allow the luck factored into this month to work its way through to you. September encourages you to showcase your individuality, to stand out rather than fit in, and to respond with wisdom and a knowing that is beyond ordinary. That's pretty special.

Your best responses for September
- There's a karmic element here, give only of your best.
- Avoid rushing to respond, give yourself time to think first.
- Be choosy, accept only what is good for you.
- Be intuitively guided.
- Choose who you want in your life.

October in a SEVEN Personal Year Cycle

A feeling of emotional stability will aid you as you step into October's push for a more authoritative demeanour in your responses to Life. And yet you can also sense that more may be expected from you than your heart wants to give. You cannot afford to be sentimental now. Situations call for sound management, to be handled by someone who can handle issues as well as people. A sense of fairness and balance needs to take precedence over emotional reaction. This does not mean that care goes out the window, but that it is more purposeful and effective. It's a busy month, with lots to keep you on your toes, including scenarios connected to property or the family home, such as buying, selling, repairing, renovating or relocating. It may also be that some of this is going on in your mind as a thought process for what you'd like to do rather than in actuality. Remember to check all documents for accuracy.

It is both fair and reasonable for you expect those in your life to do their share. Do not even muse about doing everything yourself. For sure, responsibilities may be there, but so also is the need for you to supervise and delegate. When issues land in your corner, include those involved in the process of arriving at a favourable solution for all concerned. Maintaining your composure is paramount, so refuse to lose your cool. This month calls you to deal with the situation assertively, not aggressively, not emotionally. October encourages you to base your responses on a rational and sound perspective. It's the intellect assigned to take charge over the emotions, even if the feelings of those involved need to be considered. Avoid a bossy, know-it-all attitude. Your stamina and ability to bounce back may be given a workout during October. Take care of your health by balancing commitments with rest and social connections.

Your best responses for October
- Balance authority with generosity and care.
- Showcase your humanitarian side.
- The domestic scene may be more demanding than lovable, but deal with it lovingly.
- Show them how to do it rather than doing it for them.
- Remember that charity starts at home.

November in a SEVEN Personal Year Cycle

You can expect certain things to wind up this month. This may be a project that you have been working on that reaches your anticipated finish date, or it may even be something reaching a close or conclusion as a matter of course. Some of these finalities will be from your own choosing, others may come from Life itself. These events may not necessarily be of a practical or physical nature, they may come from deep within you and manifest in your mind as an ending to a certain attitude or situation. If there's something no longer sustainable in your life, now's the time to release it, particularly any mental or emotional clutter that keeps you in struggle and survival mode instead of live and thrive mode. If there's not even a little joy in it, let it go.

There's love and celebration in November's energy, as well as drama. Immerse yourself in this universal energy that encourages you to see your connectedness to all things. This is the kind of love which does not harm. You may not be free to follow your heart in all you want to do, but rest assured, help will come through friends and loved ones who will assist you in any way they can, for fun as well as needs. In all this, your Seven PYC may ask you to take a step back and allow others to make their own choices about what to leave behind. This is a month when feelings run deep; for your part make sure they don't go so deep that you lose yourself. Avoid feelings of confusion or apprehension, especially if the changes that come to you are not of your choosing. Your Seven PYC is not about material improvement but about soul development. Its focus is on spiritual expansion and moving towards a higher level of consciousness. November encourages you to demonstrate empathy, acceptance and giving without expectation. High End stuff – the challenging, the beautiful and the loving.

Your best responses for November
- See Life's beauty more than its ugliness.
- Refuse to mix with small-minded people.
- Reminisce, but not for too long.
- Accept what is and look forward to what can be.
- Don't push for anything, November's energy is in receiving mode.

December in a SEVEN Personal Year Cycle

December brings fresh ideas and new contacts. The heaviness of your Seven PYC gives way to renewed mental creativity and business stimulation. For sure, you may feel like going full steam ahead, the ideas and plans circling your mind space are in operation mode, not rest mode. It might be wise, though, to check out your PYC for January and February in your Eight PYC. Is it in accord with what you want to do now, with your eagerness, or is it preferable to wait? If the coming months allow you the opportunity to keep moving with December's plans, then all is well. If not, then it may be wiser and safer to plan more and do less.

Look at where you are in your life and take care of any matters that call for a re-adjustment, or perhaps scrapping altogether. But do so with an eye to the future, to what you see in the months and years ahead. Take time to plan for what you want, for what you envision. If you are considering a holiday make sure that all plans are secure to enable a worry-free break. The Christmas season will keep you moving and doing – entertaining, making decisions, buying gifts and planning for family and friends. December includes loved ones, even if at times they can be more demanding than lovable. If you are feeling scattered, stop and re-organise, ground yourself. Bring in more structure and less haste. Give yourself all the time needed to get the groundwork established. Whether with family or business in mind, attend to the mundane work stuff as well as the lighter more creative stuff. If you can manage to marry up these two elements you will achieve so much more than if you try to avoid one or neglect the other. December encourages you to execute your plans with proficiency and accuracy to ensure freedom from tasks and duties spilling over into your vacation time.

Your best responses for December
- Attend to family-related matters with consideration and love.
- Take time to think.
- Resolve any problems creatively as well as realistically.
- Celebrate Life with those you love.
- Help others be more self-sufficient.

Eight
Personal Year Cycle

The EIGHT Personal Year Cycle brings experiences intended to hone and polish the following qualities and areas of life –

Drive, Ambition, Authority, Power, Recognition, Organisation, Strength, Character Building, Balance, Purpose, Expansion, Business Ability.

Its mandate is to prompt, encourage and at times push you to live these qualities to the very best of your ability in positive mode, and in so doing promote and sustain a constant state of evolving and becoming the whole and truly unique person you were born to be.

The EIGHT Personal Year Cycle

This year intends to add a definite sense of authority and purpose in your stride; this is your power year! Personal, financial and business interests will have you re-thinking and reorganising your plans and expectations with an aim towards improvement. Dealings with property or business, money, renovations, repairs, buying, selling, or simply planning to do this, whether for yourself or others, will keep you busy. Decide what you want to do and be realistic about your ability, your skills and your desired accomplishments. For sure, this is the time for you to go after what you want, but understand that you must also have what it takes to do so. For example, you might want to buy a large family property, but if you are not sufficiently cashed-up to do so, you will get yourself into trouble. This scenario doesn't necessarily mean you need to scrap the purchase, it might mean considering a smaller, more affordable property. This is a time for realism to exceed optimism. It's not about waiting for that something to land in your lap without effort. Are you prepared to keep going when the going gets tough? If so, then place your talents and skills on the market. This is your year for recognition. For your part, be sure you are recognised for the good you do, not its opposite. If you feel you have contributed to the max and it warrants a pay increase or a promotion, state your case – but be businesslike about it, be factual not mousy. Assert your expectations and go for it with a genuine confidence.

Interesting people and experiences are part of the year. This will be a busy one, demanding much of your time and energy. Invest in healthy eating, lots of fresh air and exercise. The push for ambitious projects and accomplishment will give you little time to rest, so it's important that you balance action with resting and relaxing. Towards the end of this Eight PYC, Life intends to have you well established where it matters. To ensure the success offered, maintain a serious confidence and contribute to projects that benefit others as well as yourself. Don't give up on your goals when Life tests your mettle, but rather re-energise your sense of purpose and direction for what you have planned. Keep at it, keep going for gold, even in the face of adversity. The Eight PYC will test your strength, character and endurance, to see if you fit the bill, so to speak, with what it is preparing to offer you. It is not a year for weakness; it demands one hundred per cent effort on your part if it is to deliver the success it promises.

Much is offered in an Eight PYC, but much more is also expected. It is a time when you can feel driven, a time when the push to do and to accomplish is far stronger than anything less. In all this, the year offers you a sense of authority. The question is, can you handle it? Can you put it to use or is it more overwhelming than empowering? If you feel overwhelmed, pull back and re-organise. Take stock of your work and home commitments and rearrange them in ways that allow you a degree of improvement and accomplishment. Delegate if necessary. The energy of the year is just as intent on polishing up and honing your skills in good management and leadership as it is intent on hard work. Sometimes you can excel at what you do and rightly expect to be rewarded for your effort and then find that someone else gets the prize. This sometimes happens to test your resilience. If this happens, for sure you will take to your corner for a while, for refuge from the unexpected hurt, but do not linger there too long and miss out on Life's other offerings – which may only be a few feet away from what you wanted.

Your best responses in an EIGHT Personal Year Cycle
- Be discreet where love affairs are concerned, yours or someone else's.
- Make time for family and maintaining good health.
- Each time you trip up, get up again and get going again.
- A chance to demonstrate courage, take it.
- Think like a business person.
- Be willing to include others on your journey up the ladder.

- Avoid complaining, Life is not listening.
- Feel the sense of empowerment the year offers and use it.
- Join groups and community projects.
- For maximum results, immerse your spiritual side with all things material.

January in a EIGHT Personal Year Cycle

Expect to see some plans reach maturity during January. This may involve marked decisions regarding property, perhaps even the family home, with the possibility of selling or of negotiating some sort of property settlement which will eventuate in a rearrangement of previous plans. Maybe it's a thought process, something you're thinking about. It may not be what's in your heart to do, but more what you feel is the better way. This may more than likely be connected with situations that had to be dealt with last year (in your Seven PYC) and necessary to enable you to move forward with your new objectives. It is understandable that you may feel confused and uncertain, but do your utmost to push for the best possible outcome. Take your time to consider your options. Your feelings might tell you one thing and your head another. Above all, seek to improve your standing, your security. Be encouraged, as once you have re-established clarity of mind you will be able to look ahead to future possibilities. Take the time to organise and prioritise your activities as a basis for your intended plans.

Disappointment may be experienced when something you were expecting to go ahead this month does not eventuate. Regardless of who is responsible, you may need to handle it. Remember your Eight PYC is intent on polishing up your strength and business ability. Take care to address all legal documents with executive accuracy before signing. Even though you are in a year of business, power and authority, January's energy calls for compassion and letting go of certain things. Sometimes we might take a small loss to enable a future gain. Take heart, join with those who hold a little piece of your heart, with those who share similar interests, to celebrate and enjoy each other's company.

Your best responses for January
- Avoid going too deep with what you feel.
- Settle problems to enable you to move forward with confidence.
- Let go of what is stopping you from moving towards a better future.
- Feel the love around you more than anything else.
- Be selective – spend time with people who have good intentions towards you.

February in an EIGHT Personal Year Cycle

The energy has changed and you can almost feel that life is giving you a fresh start. Your emotions are steadier and it's your mind that's taken charge now. Your focus is on the ideas and plans going on in your head as you try to think of ways to materialise your dreams and ideas, whether small or grand. For sure, this is an excellent time for you to work on your goals, on what you can see as doable in future months, in future years even. It is exciting, yes, but you must base it all and prepare it all on a sound business perspective. Use the creative intelligence and foresight available to you now as you envision all that you wish to accomplish by the end of your Eight PYC, whether a new kitchen or a new business, a palatial home or a tiny house. The time is right for planning something new, or something new taken from the established and given a more updated and fresher perspective.

Family matters cannot be escaped, so play your part without feeling frustrated about other people's inadequacies. Show loved ones how to be more independent rather than doing things for them because it's quicker for you. Encourage those in your life to slowly move out of their comfort zone, to show more initiative. Mix courage with patience as you move forward with your intentions and wait for your ideas to take hold and become a reality. This is a beginning time in creative planning which will come to fruition in the months ahead. Deal with responsibilities graciously and be willing to take care of loved ones in need with calm and logic. Past issues and future expectations need to be handled with efficiency and love. Look out for the offer that may materialise and which will both please you and inspire you to keep moving in a forward direction.

Your best responses for February
- Take charge of your life.
- Include leadership with care for others.
- Use foresight to encourage you to keep moving ahead.
- See the good in others more than their weaknesses.
- Success is there but Life is asking you to chase it if you want it.

March in an EIGHT Personal Year Cycle

March will find you rather busy as a great deal of what happens will come through the involvement of others. Many of the little insecurities will be behind you now and you will sense a feeling of satisfaction and happiness in how things are working out. Even so, do not feel that you have to rely just on yourself. Do talk to people who can assist you, as this month's energy leans towards putting support systems in place with those who are skilled and knowledgeable, as well as with those who can offer emotional support. Invite others into your space, into your life. The Eight PYC is extrovert in its nature and so encourages mixing and forming friendships and alliances. March carries an energy of opposites which can have you feeling somewhat indecisive, not being quite certain which way to move. With this in mind it's best to observe situations before responding, then consider whether it's best to push ahead and take charge or to stay put and play your part as a member of the team.

In all this you may still experience some upset in a business or personal relationship. The best approach is one of composure and confidence mixed with kindness and a win-win intention for all concerned. And then give it space to work itself out. Keep a positive attitude even if something that cannot be changed at present is annoying or frustrating. Understand that the decision you are considering regarding an issue or person is best kept to yourself for now. This is a people month, so enjoy time spent together with family and friends. Be open, as some relationships call to be loosened or strengthened.

Your best responses for March

- Avoid being critical or apprehensive if you experience opposition.
- Patience is important now as anything else could upset your well laid plans.
- When dealing with others, tact and diplomacy will take you further than forceful convincing.
- Listen and watch before responding. Read between and behind what is obvious.
- Be able to discern whether it's best to step up or to stay put.

April in an EIGHT Personal Year Cycle

April brings conditions which allow you to focus more on your personal needs, even though commitments and responsibilities still need to be met. Express your feelings, albeit sensibly, and take advantage of this month's energy to envision future possibilities. Look ahead to what can be, without allowing the practical, or the challenges to dissect your enthusiasm or your optimism. This month has a positive energy which allows you to feel the inspiration that is very much connected to what you are trying to achieve. It allows a bird's-eye view of what is yet to be taken on board to ensure success and happiness. In all this, though, do not allow your healthy optimism to misinterpret your reality. With emotions taking centre stage, take care to not wear your heart on your sleeve, as they say. Also, keep in mind that others may not share the same enthusiasm as you do, but do not interpret this as them not being happy for you. It may be that they are experiencing something more mundane.

Indulge yourself a little this month, as your bank balance allows of course. For sure, there's an element of extravagance throughout April which can have you leaning towards extra spending. In all this, be sure to make time for those you call friends. Show them how much you appreciate them by being attentive when they need your support. Any activity along artistic and creative lines will add to your enjoyment and success. Take the step if the new idea or new direction offers promise. At the same time, take care to not give away any ideas or plans that could be useful in the future. April is a good month for communicating your feelings, for giving and taking in lectures, going to the theatre, for participating in cultural and social activities generally.

Your best responses for April
- Avoid feeling scattered, ground yourself.
- Romance draws you in – a person, or something creative or artistic that you love.
- Avoid magnifying your sensitivity, while considering the sensitivity of those in your life.
- Maintain mental stability and use good judgement in your decision making.
- Have fun, but keep your feet on terra firma.

May in an EIGHT Personal Year Cycle

Throughout May, you will be encouraged to get down to bedrock. Sure, you may at times feel somewhat boxed in, and perhaps even feel that you are not getting anywhere, that things are moving way too slowly for you. May is intentionally a slow-moving month, and if you are able to involve yourself in what is important, in what needs doing, you will find the month to be one of significance and one which becomes a stepping stone to future achievement and success. May asks you to look at your life squarely. To see both people and situations as they really are. It's accepting that circumstances, or what you discover may not be to your liking, are all the more reason for implementing good management skills and putting everything in perspective. This is necessary if you are to know exactly where your starting point is. Only by doing this can you set plans in motion for what you want and create a sound base to build on for something lasting.

Money may be a little tight at this time and a re-arrangement of plans may be needed in order to meet the practical and economic energy that May carries. It's important that you deal with any legal requirements professionally and astutely. For sure, the focus of the month is more about life's practical stuff, more about what needs to be done rather than what you would like to be doing. And yet for this very reason you need to purposely slot in time for fun and enjoyment, for things that make you happy. Avoid overdoing in any area and maintain good health and a positive mood. Know that the work and effort you are putting in now will free up more of your time later. Family commitments and responsibilities are present; for your part blend them with social outings and enjoyment.

Your best responses for May
- Refuse to get stuck in a rut – keep moving with purpose.
- Bring more structure into your life – get organised.
- Roll up your sleeves, you will get so much done this month.
- Be prepared to do more for others than others do for you.
- Enjoy being part of family and community.

June in an EIGHT Personal Year Cycle

June brings a lighter workload in the practical sense, though its energy moves in active mode nonetheless. It's not a time which is at ease with solitude and going it alone. If getting out and about physically is not for you, then perhaps you can connect via electronics and social media. Take the time to meet new people, also to catch up with some you have not seen for a while. It's a month which brings change and opportunity. So, dress up, show up and check out what Life has to offer. There will be chances to promote yourself and/or your area of expertise, so consider what is available for workability and potential success. Make changes if they foster improvement. June's energy will have you on the move, whether locally or further afield, for business, pleasure or perhaps a combination of the two. Know that in all this, however, it's not a time to take uncalculated risks.

Allow yourself to surrender to the energy and enthusiasm the month offers. For sure, there is much to do, but refuse to fall into a state of doing without accomplishing. By all means mingle, enjoy, have fun, but be sure to also make people connections which can help you to materialise your plans and ideas. Refuse to get caught up in disagreements as June's energy can have you quick to retaliate before thinking whether it's the wisest move. Be self-aware, as you do not want to create arguments or problems where none are warranted. Carry out your work with patience and precision, take care of the little things that you may think unimportant, they can sometimes make a big difference. Attend to any paperwork with a clear mind and be certain of your requirements and expectations before signing on the dotted line. Business opportunities may come to you through partnerships or through others generally. Work as part of a team to maximise improvement. Mix, mingle and enjoy being a part of Life.

Your best responses for June
- Enjoy the feeling of freedom that June's energy offers.
- Talk to people, don't wait for them to start a conversation.
- Be confident and assertive, but also include gentler qualities.
- Look for opportunities on offer, catch one or two.
- Be aware of the sensitivity and spirituality in June's energy – see its potential for good.

July in an EIGHT Personal Year Cycle

Prepare yourself for the duties and responsibilities that July deems to be yours to handle. Take heart, though, for it's not intended to be all work and no play. You will have it in you to carry out what is expected without losing out on what you want to do for your own needs and personal enjoyment. There's an element of care which runs through the month, the opportunity to help someone who relies on you. Know that accepting and giving of your help willingly, graciously, will bring its rewards. Also know that an attitude that is fixed or selfish will not work for you this month. Expect issues on the domestic front to make their way to you for a resolution. The best way to deal with these is by negotiation and adjustments. Consider any information that comes to light. Be fair and just without being judgemental, without taking sides.

Family, friends and community affairs will be in focus as your Eight PYC invites you be caring without going into overdrive. July's intention is to maximise the quality of relationships – however, it's important to note that love, whether given genuinely or not, can determine a strengthening or loosening of the connection. Everything under the umbrella of family takes centre stage this month. Play your part without restricting anyone else's freedom of choice where it matters and avoid getting weighed down by taking on more than July intends. Children will be a source of joy, with the possibility of care and challenges thrown in. In all this, business plans and options are set to maintain momentum and money should not be an issue, though it's not a time to overindulge in unnecessary purchases. Generally, you will find this to be a rewarding month, with good times and celebrations intermingled with responsibilities. Affairs of the heart will feature during July, yours or someone you know.

Your best responses for July
- Take care of any health issues, yours or someone else's.
- Praise more and reprimand less.
- Avoid focusing on what's missing, appreciate what is, what you have.
- You may not be in control, but you can still encourage, inspire and enjoy the accolades.
- Combine commitments with social interaction and lots of love.

August in an EIGHT Personal Year Cycle

Our mind plays a huge part in what we do and how we feel. If we allow it, our mind can have us believing all sorts of untruths about ourselves. During August this is particularly true as this month's energy is more introspective than out there. Should you choose to go at Life like it's your way or none at all, then you may find that you will accomplish absolutely zero – or next to that! With the right frame of mind, though, you can come out winning. August asks you to raise the bar, to respond to experiences not emotionally or intellectually but from a position of wisdom, trust and understanding. Your achievement and success rate will depend more on what you think than what you do. Look within yourself for back-up this month, to your Higher Self.

This is the time for you to step up, to elevate your view of Life and all it offers. From that elevated standing point you will be able to see more, much more clearly. It's time to loosen the controls, state what you want and then release the outcome to the field of possibilities. The time is right to pursue study, reading, quiet arts and crafts, music and anything that will expand your mind and consciousness.

August offers you the chance to hone and polish your character as much as a hobby or work area you love. There is an element of disruption through the month, so allow yourself more time to get to any important meetings or appointments. If things do not go according to your plans, see this for what it is – Life asking you to trust that you are being looked after, even though you may not be able to see it. Release any resentment and leave anything less than love and understanding on the shelf. Keep fit and healthy, add some personal quality time to your agenda or daily list of 'must dos' – or better still, take a holiday!

Your best responses for August
- Avoid force or pushing for what you want, it won't work.
- Emotional responses won't work, wisdom and understanding will.
- Step into the flow of Life, be intuitively guided.
- Offer least resistance to change.
- Spend time with friends who understand you.

September in an EIGHT Personal Year Cycle

You will welcome the steadier feel that comes with September, even if at times you may sense that you are really not in control. And yet, this month's experiences are intent on honing and polishing your leadership qualities and your ability to resolve problems. This is the high point to your Eight PYC. Take heart, for September is geared to reward you for all your hard work and past effort. Financial improvement is also on the table. In all this, though, do not waver in your effort and lose sight of what is to come. This month's energy, its mandate, asks that you make decisions with the guidance of your intellect and reasoning powers and keep any emotional responses for another time. Get yourself into business mode and make your decisions from a position of objectivity and logic. Clarity of mind is important now, as you begin to see the possibilities waiting to be taken to the next level of accomplishment. There is much to do now. You may even feel ambitiously driven to do more.

Finding an equilibrium or balance is paramount. Avoid being too set on what you want to do. Though September is not about your personal wants, you will benefit personally once you realise and accept the extent of help those in your life are prepared to offer. You may find yourself making a decision or reaching a conclusion about something that has been on your mind. This is may be connected to past events, perhaps having to do with a love affair or personal relationship. The courage to *do* sits in challenge position and may need coaxing out of its idleness. Let go of what you must, of what is genuinely no longer yours. Make any necessary changes without feelings of resentment. In doing this you will be able to enjoy the success and compliments wrapped up in September's energy cycle.

Your best responses for September
- The buck stops with you, so assume authority.
- Be strong, be vigilant, be reasonable, be loving, be calm, be balanced.
- Refrain from going at top speed and depleting your stamina and health.
- Allow intuitive guidance to filter into your reasoning process.
- Showcase your character, your strength and your talents.

October in an EIGHT Personal Year Cycle

Feelings dominate this month, along with a more pensive and reflective mood. When we have feelings taking centre stage, drama is sure to follow, but for you any melodrama is best avoided. October is intent on winding things down rather than winding them up, which presents the opportunity for you to put an end to, conclude, or change something. Be aware as problems may arise between yourself and others. The situation will call for understanding and empathy on your part, regardless of who's at fault. Take the time needed to ensure certainty about what you want the outcome to be. If you are considering ending a relationship, whether personal or work related, then be certain that this is what you really want before making your final move.

Look at any business projects that are not possible now and pack them away for another time. Do the same with any 'stuff' that is overwhelming you, with anything that is taking up valuable space in your head or in your heart and is keeping you stuck. If Life deems something to be, then let it be with love and compassion. October brings experiences for you to fine-tune your capacity to give and receive love and understanding. The demonstration of these two high-end qualities is essential in your interaction with others as well as in any decisions you make. There's a chance someone close will pour out their heart to you; for sure, take the time to listen, but be clear that it is not your call to give advice. Reassure them, though, that you will remain a friend regardless of any decision they make. Use the deep feeling in October's energy to see the beautiful around you. Celebrate with those you love and be grateful for the positives that come to you.

Your best responses for October
- If change is on your mind, be certain it's what you want before initiating.
- Stamp 'closed' on what is no longer useful, wanted or possible in your life.
- Enjoy the recognition, even if it's a simple 'thank you'.
- Release any resentment with love. Then move on.
- Feel the awe of Life's grandeur and know that you are an integral part of it all. Love that!

November in an EIGHT Personal Year Cycle

There is a great deal going on in your mind and much of it has to do with taking charge of your life. Perhaps you have been reluctant to do so, for which you may have had your reasons, but Life knows that what you need is more important to you than what you may want. This month's energy is intended to encourage and even push you to take control over your life, even in the midst of responsibilities and expectations linked to others. Because they also have to be considered, as they also play a part in what needs to be done. November's expectation is clear – if you cannot make decisions, resolve problems and have courage to take the lead for yourself, then who will, and when will you be ready for the bigger role of leading those in your care? Though there is still some degree of uncertainty in the air, you will, however, be glad and be encouraged by the clarity of mind that now seems to come to you.

Give yourself a chance to prioritise the important stuff. For sure, you will feel the excitement as life urges you to move ahead with your plans. But in all this, November asks that you to show those in your life that they can rely on you. Someone will ask for your support, perhaps a family member. Be gracious in your giving; don't make them feel they are imposing on you or your time. Understand that maintaining your individuality and personal space does not translate into permission for shirking your commitments and responsibilities, even if at times you feel held back by what is expected from you. Or even by what you expect from yourself. November's energy offers you the foresight and courage needed to keep moving forward with your plans, with what you want to do, with what can be achieved and with where you envision your tomorrows to take you.

Your best responses for November
- Take care of your health and wellbeing.
- Be gracious in all you do and say.
- Take the lead with authority and gratitude.
- Accept responsibilities, but at the same time maintain your individuality.
- Consider something different, a new approach perhaps.

December in an EIGHT Personal Year Cycle

There is a spiritual element running through December. Life brings experiences which offer the chance to rise above the ordinary and to truly shine in some way. A mini-crisis can be avoided by being more understanding, even though you may not agree, or you find yourself in a situation that is uncomfortable and not of your choosing. The incidents and issues that surface now are intended to encourage good character and the ability to see beyond any issue. If you are to stand out from the rest, if you are to be the more enlightened one, then you must be self-aware and respond only from your best self. In all this, if someone chooses more distance between you, then let it be with love and good wishes for them as well as yourself. Remember your Eight PYC is one which is set to hone and polish your strength and resilience in all areas of your life.

You may feel a sense of restlessness and a longing to do what you want to do, while at the same time feeling that something is holding you back and not allowing you the complete freedom to be all of you. Do not be headstrong or critical now. Pull back from quick responses. Ask yourself if you will get the best outcome by stepping up and taking charge or by cooperating. It's in knowing you have a choice and opting for the one that will benefit all concerned that you will make your mark, that will allow you to feel that inner power and harmony. Make time to connect with others as you celebrate the Christmas festivities with those you love. It's a busy time with lots to do, but if you feel alone in the midst of it all, don't take to your corner for too long. Be a part of the joy and generosity intended at this time.

Your best responses for December
- Enjoy social outings with friends as well as time on your own.
- December brings the chance to trim or reinforce some relationships.
- Refuse to be self-absorbed, share the joy and goodwill.
- Make time to do some of the things you love with someone you love.
- Accept more invitations to celebrate.

Nine
Personal Year Cycle

The NINE Personal Year Cycle brings experiences intended to hone and polish the following qualities and areas of life –

The Link between Humanity and Divinity, Philanthropy, Artistry and Creativity, Love, Compassion, Understanding, Forgiveness, Completion, Deep Feeling, Generosity, Impressionability, Perfection.

Its mandate is to prompt, encourage and at times push you to live these qualities to the very best of your ability in positive mode, and in so doing promote and sustain a constant state of evolving and becoming the whole and truly unique person you were born to be.

The NINE Personal Year Cycle

You are now preparing to conclude your Personal Major Time Cycle of nine years, with a brand new nine-year cycle commencing with your next birthday. This year is like the final chapter of a book. It contains conclusions, endings, drama, release, forgiveness, love, compassion, success, deep feelings … A whole gamut of experiences culminating in one, a collective of the past eight years with this as the final act. What feelings will it conjure up in you? For sure, you will experience a mix of agony, ecstasy and everything in between. Feel it all and be grateful, even if some things tug at your heart-strings a little too much. The Nine PYC is not one for chasing after what you want. It is a time for giving and receiving, a time for practising and polishing Life's high-end qualities of loving without strings, understanding when others misunderstand, forgiveness, compassion and empathy. Your Nine PYC intends to give these qualities a workout as it encourages you towards a higher level of consciousness. Will you accept and receive its rewards, or will you resist?

This is not a time for you to be starting something, nor to be forcing any issues. It's a year for reflecting on what has been, on how you travelled over the past eight years, and on where you want to go when this PYC reaches completion. Who and what will you leave behind? This includes the material stuff as well as emotional ties. Be specific about this. Consider clearing away all things that are no longer necessary, that no longer function, or that no longer make your heart sing. Consider the people in your life too. Who is for you and who is against you, who both cries and laughs with you? Who wants you to succeed and thrive? As you can see, you have much to think about, much on which to ponder.

Perhaps this year will mark the completion of a study or a project you have been working on. It can be like the grand finale, after many years of application. Sometimes Life itself makes the decision to bring about endings over which we have no control. Other times the decision is made by us. For sure, when you can respond to what Life brings with understanding, compassion, tolerance and forgiveness, you open the way for rewards of love, fulfilment and financial improvement. The Nine PYC offers all when your responses are as High End as its offerings. It's not easy to forgive some things, some people, so begin with a sincere *willingness* to forgive. Release any hate or resentment and invite peace to take its place.

Should you feel a pull away from established areas of your life and a turning towards new interests, do not allow this to concern you. This is part of the transition from the old to the new. Matters of the heart will feature this year, joy intermingled with sadness. What you feel will be felt more deeply this year, which can lower your moods. Take care to not go too deep. Be aware, as your energy can be magnetic during this cycle, connecting with other energies unknowingly, so mix only with those who want good for you. With those who are broad-minded. Make the most of the big breaks as life seeks to reward you as a conclusion to the courage and go-get-it attitude you demonstrated last year. Monetary gain is according to how you responded to Life in past years. According to how well you lived and responded to previous time cycle mandates. There is no limit to what can be accomplished – this is a year for charity, philanthropy, art, creativity, business, travel and cultural interests. Immerse yourself in all that is beautiful, in all that is love and consciously release all that is less.

Your best responses in a NINE Personal Year Cycle
- Clear out your wardrobe, your storage, do away with those things you have been holding onto 'just in case'.
- Let go of anything that is not necessary or that you no longer want in your life.
- Consider loosening or cutting ties with anyone who does not have good intentions for you. Do it with love.
- Take care of your health, especially your emotional and mental health.
- Avoid making money an issue this year.

- Work with the intention of success for others as well as yourself to attract greater rewards.
- Make 'love, peace and joy' your default mantra.
- Opportunities come to you, consider them, but do not start new ventures, leave that for your next PYC.
- Respond to the year's experiences only from your best, as Life prepares you for a fresh start next birthday.
- Feel the pulse of Life – all of it. Be grateful for all that is good and be willing to release all that is less.

January in a NINE Personal Year Cycle

If you feel the impulse to be up and doing things this month, keep in mind that the time is right to start winding things down, not start things up. Though January's energy is geared towards creative thinking and can have you venturing into new territory, it's about planning for the new, not implementing something new. Consider the viability of your ideas – do they fit in with your plans, or are changes needed? Money matters surface, but avoid making that an issue. Look to the future as you take the initiative in clearing up what is no longer important or of value in your life. The future you want may seem like a long way off and perhaps you are not quite certain how it will turn out, but do not let that trouble you. Think things through clearly, put them on paper and see if it's what you want.

Take charge of your life as you decide what you wish to take into your future and what you want to leave behind. Selling or giving away things that are past their use-by date for you will free up space which can be useful later. Take a good look at your relationships, professional and personal, and decide where they are taking you. January is for resolving issues, for coming up with a new approach, for viewing something with different eyes. In all this be sure to exercise tolerance and compassion in all your decisions. Avoid giving in to anger or regret over what you should have done or not done. Keep doubt and apprehension under control as you plan which part of your life is moving into your tomorrow and which you will leave behind. January gives you a peek into your One PYC. Feel the excitement but refrain from moving into anything new.

Your best responses for January
- Look back over your life and be content with all you have experienced, even if there are some things you wish you could change.
- Look at past events and come up with ideas for building on the positives.
- Respond with your intellect – assertively but not aggressively.
- Manage your finances with reason, not emotion.
- Make time for creative thinking, birth some new ideas.

February in a NINE Personal Year Cycle

As you venture into the activities of the month you will be comforted by the reassurance, help and inspiration that come from significant others in your life. There will be times when you will want to withdraw from life's busyness, to seek refuge in the recesses of your mind, but do refrain from settling there. For sure, this can be a month of fragile emotions if you give way to sensitive feelings. You may be privy to information related to the past you did not wish to hear. Let it go. Release it and do not look back, move past it. Refuse to give it energy. It is important that you maintain the spiritual channel open as you come to terms with the realities of life. Understand that even though others are there to help you, time is still needed before the finals of this Nine PYC can be fully realised.

Annoyance and upset can surface over someone's unfair actions or interference in your life. But it is in your best interest to be tactful and gentle in your responses this month. If you must, get another person's opinion on the matter concerning you, but be certain that they are objective and not personally involved. February will bring its fair share of social outings and people interaction to be enjoyed, perhaps with the inclusion of friends you don't see too often. Make time for the care and duties of others in the midst of your own activities this month. February can bring a mixture of emotions – from sadness to joy and all that is in between. For your part, maintain a closer connection to the lighter, happier side. Play your part to the best of your ability and know that in all this your gentleness and care will be appreciated and rewarded.

Your best responses for February
- Respond with a quiet confidence.
- Mix with others without trading your individuality.
- A chance to shine brightly, but only if you can rise above the nitty gritty some people are stuck on.
- Allow into your space only those who genuinely care about you.
- Be gentle, be kind, be tactful, but do not be a weakling.

March in a NINE Personal Year Cycle

As you move into March you will be aware of a lighter, less serious and more optimistic energy. You may even feel the haze of uncertainty begin to clear. You will feel inspired as you come up with new ideas regarding your future. Friends are important this month and you are encouraged by the admiration that is communicated to you. Chances are you will generally feel more positive and upbeat about your life. For sure, commitments and responsibilities linger on and do take up some of your time, but this doesn't have to exclude catching up with friends and having fun. So be sure to factor that into your schedule too.

When the affairs of others annoy or frustrate you, refuse to get caught up in any negative emotions. See this for what it is – Life giving you a practice run at honing and polishing the tolerance and compassion scripted into your Nine PYC. Pay particular attention to how you express your ideas and feelings, keep your intentions positive. With emotions ruling over your reasoning during March, it's important to not communicate anything that can land you in hot water. You will be pleased with the suggestion or offer that comes to you that allows you to see promise in something that is close to your heart. All in all March proves to be a positive month paving the way for self-expression, social interaction and friendships. Make the most of the new interest or new opportunity presented to you. Be kind and lend an ear to friends who may be caught up in affairs of the heart.

Your best responses for March
- A month with a focus on friendly interaction, best met with happiness in mind.
- Loved ones will also want a little piece of you, say 'yes' with a smile that shows you mean it.
- Avoid gossip – creating it, listening to it, or spreading it.
- Add a creative flair to all you do this month.
- Be as a child at heart – bring some form of play into life's seriousness.

April in a NINE Personal Year Cycle

April's energy carries a more serious tone as Life encourages you to look at your situation more squarely. You will come to the realisation that things cannot continue as they have been in the past. But for sure, this is not a time for panic – it is a time for economic truth, for adjusting your spending so that it is more in line with your income and cash flow. You may feel a little boxed-in as April steers you towards settling your accounts payable, some possibly before the month's end. While you would prefer to be doing more of what you like and being more free than serious, if you make the necessary changes now this in turn will clear the way towards less duties and adding more freedom and independence in the months and years ahead. You will need to be practical and economical now. Do not allow impatience or discouragement to upset this grounding necessary for future benefits.

The feeling of restriction or that it's all up to you is not just in your mind, as matters surface which perhaps you have been avoiding or not wanting to see. Both emotional and practical changes are necessary now to improve living conditions. Look at the options available to you. It won't help you to be critical, or to blame others for the situation you find yourself in. Property and legal papers may need to be considered, and if so pay attention to the details before signing. Take heart and you will find that any uncertainty will pass. There is an opportunity in April geared towards money making, if not for now then perhaps for the future. Consider it for viability.

Your best responses for April
- Be more serious-minded than anything else. Be resourceful.
- Take care to not be flippant with any changes. Make them only to put you on a more constructive base.
- The domestic scene features, so do what needs doing without feeling that too much is expected from you.
- Apply yourself more, deal with any restlessness.

May in a NINE Personal Year Cycle

Change and new experiences are intended to add enthusiasm to all you take on board this month. For sure, there's more freedom on offer, more impulse to do as you will, but in all this there's an underlying current of seriousness which asks you to be purposely practical with any intended changes. Avoid running around with your head in the air wondering where to concentrate your priorities. There is much for you to consider but take the time needed to slow your mind down long enough to centre yourself, and then remind yourself that any start is fine – just begin. The need for structure and a methodical approach is there and cannot be escaped. Giving in to half-hearted feelings for organisation and discipline in all things practical could see you missing out on the promise of improvement that May offers. Be methodical but not pedantic.

Look at what you've accomplished so far, because it's certain the progress around you will have a positive effect on you, even if you feel that getting things finished is taking forever. You will enjoy the public contact this month, which adds inspiration and a sense of exhilaration to May's offerings. Some things may not go according to plan, but that should not pose too much concern as you make the necessary changes. Family members may not agree with your intentions. They may consider your actions to be lacking in some way, not as they 'should' be. Refuse to react, to upset yourself as well as others, instead devise a way to meet your commitments without compromising your independence. There are certainly opportunities for the taking – the difficulty may lie in making up your mind about what is important to you right now. May will prove a winner when you blend innovation with structure, work with fun.

Your best responses for May

- Changes are essential, but take the time to ensure that any change brings improvement.
- Avoid being hasty, allow enough time. Do things right instead of fast.
- Bring in more structure, but not rigidity.
- Bending the rules is one thing, but breaking them can prove costly.
- Be flexible.

June in a NINE Personal Year Cycle

June is a month when emotions and feelings can overrule reason, so be aware. The month is also set to bring you some of the results you have been anticipating. Do enjoy the satisfaction that comes with these accomplishments, no matter how small, but avoid rushing things through with the desire to have everything finished and tied up. Expect this month to bring family, children and loved ones to the fore, with some decisions also involving them. You are right to feel that lots is expected from you – your charitable side, how much you are willing to do, how much you are willing to give – will be given a workout. You can be forgiven for asking yourself why this is happening, but it's far more advantageous for you to focus on your response. The one that will bring more of what you want is doing and giving, without feeling that you are being imposed upon. It's not about working or giving to exhaustion, so do draw that imaginary line and pencil in some time with a special other, a little romance perhaps, or simply spending time in friendship and fun.

There are good times to be enjoyed this month as you connect socially. But even this is something you yourself must pursue, if you want more of it. A decision may be made regarding the past, which is part of the conclusions and finalities of the year. In all this keep in mind that doing so will enable you to offload any emotional heaviness that may still be lingering. Shift your view, ease up a little and be grateful for the love and support given by those who care about you. Your happiness hormones are in challenge mode, so you will need to deliberately activate them, to express your feelings in a more light-hearted and positive way. Remind yourself to do something that makes you happy – for no other reason, just for you!

Your best responses for June
- Avoid seeing things in black and white, as good or bad.
- Stop yourself from stepping into over-care. You matter too.
- Take care of any health issues.
- Make time for your friends, for those who make you laugh out loud!
- See this as a month of connections and disconnections.

July in a NINE Personal Year Cycle

This month's energy will bring a definite yearning to spend more time on your own – away from the hustle and bustle of life's demands and expectations. And why not! July is not a time for you to take on any responsibilities apart from what is absolutely necessary. It's busy enough as it is, but you don't have to say 'yes' to everyone's requests. Say 'no' more often. Or if that feels too strong, try 'not today, maybe another day'. Choose who you want in your life right now and who you don't want. July will expect you to draw from within yourself the stuff that makes heroes and heroines and that turns any challenges into goals accomplished. And yes, you can do it! Free up your mind space, contemplate life's mysteries and slot in time to ponder those big questions that we all ask ourselves from time to time – Life's whys and why nots … its possibilities, its miracles.

The less you take on board the better. 'Easy does it' is the philosophy to adopt right now. Friends and loved ones may not understand your need for this mini-sabbatical, just let them know that you need time out to recharge your energy. It's not a lie, because your energy levels can be lower than average in a Nine PYC. Avoid getting upset over what others say, for overly sensitive feelings will not resolve anything. Your emotions may run deep as you travel down memory lane and relive past experiences through the archives of your mind. You may feel that you have lost out somewhere – and perhaps you have, but it's done. Put it behind you and have faith in the bigger picture. Take care of your health and if you can manage a couple of days away with a good friend, go for it. It could just be the missing link that connects you to that Higher Power and to that place within where your heart is at one with your soul.

Your best responses for July
- Refuse to be rushed or dictated to.
- Step alongside Life and allow Her to lead you.
- Offer least resistance, it works better than force this month.
- Showcase your gentler side.
- Avoid over-thinking, over-analysing. Acceptance will open the door.

August in a NINE Personal Year Cycle

August brings a steadying of emotions. It's nice to not feel so emotionally vulnerable, even if the deep feeling of your Nine PYC is still hovering in the background. Nonetheless, you may sense that all is not under your control, that someone else has the controls. For sure your courageous self may be in challenge mode right now, but you must ground yourself if you are to take the lead and deal with situations as they arise. August requires and expects a more determined and assured approach from you. Add a little more structure and sound management principles as you make decisions with more authority and purpose. Good judgement and a good business attitude are essential now. While money may come and go, your Nine PYC may also deliver some sort of well-deserved recognition or award. Be happy and accept this without undue concern about money at this stage.

There may be a business proposition for you to consider, one which requires you to look at it from all angles. Assess what's on offer with objectivity, weighing all the pros and cons. For sure, this is not something that you need to tackle on your own. Consider discussing it with those who can offer good advice and remember to also consider the success of others who are involved. Stop yourself from pushing too hard to make it happen. Understand that this opportunity is one of many that you will be able to use as a building block towards future success and achievement. Tie up any unfinished business and attend to any documents with a clear mind. Friends may involve you in their affairs; take the time to lend an ear, support them, but do not get involved. All in all, August is a month which gives you an assuring glimpse into possible future achievements.

Your best responses for August
- Respond to what Life brings from a business perspective.
- If someone else is running your show, you might need to remind them that it is *your* show.
- Be quietly confident, but avoid tunnel vision.
- Bring more balance into all you do and pay attention to your health.
- You may feel the drive to accomplish, but resist starting something new.

September in a NINE Personal Year Cycle

September carries a double measure of the emotional intensity of your Nine PYC. But it also carries a double measure of opportunity for you to be outstanding in some way. Progress has been made, you can see this, and yet some feelings about past events still tug at you. It may be difficult but it's important that you do not dwell on past events that you wish had been different. Regret is a word to be left out of your vocabulary and deleted from your psyche. Even now the actions of others may upset you and add unwanted drama in your life, when all you want is harmony. You may feel unsteady, as though you're not sure what to do or not to do, but perhaps you can begin by releasing what does not bring you happiness and purpose.

For sure, it may be difficult to express compassion and forgiveness as you recall past hurts and negative experiences, but the time is right for you to accept the past for what it was. Perhaps you can begin with a willingness to forgive and release past hurts. In this way you allow yourself the freedom and self-love to move forward. So consciously offload any painful memories that have kept you from being happy. Make the choice to take charge of your life and start living more fully, completely, with intention. Once you do this, you open yourself up to receive Life's rewards of love, joy and celebration that are so much a part of your Nine PYC. In addition, it will open the way for September's energy of business and financial improvement to shift closer to reality. This month brings an opportunity to bring people together in social, traditional or cultural ways. Mix with others and celebrate, party, have fun. Celebrate life!

Your best responses for September
- Say 'yes to more party invitations and celebrations.
- Wind up what is no longer useful or functional in your life.
- Leave small-minded people outside, mix only with people who have expanded visions for humanity.
- Express your feelings and emotions – feel them, and then release them.
- Make money work for you, not burden you.

October in a NINE Personal Year Cycle

You will sense that emotions and feelings are not so dictatorial this month. Their sometimes overwhelming nature is beginning to lift as clarity of mind opens the way to mental creativity. New ideas will begin to move in along with what you wish to accomplish, what you desire to do. It is still not advisable to push fully ahead with your new plans, but plan you must! This month will bring it all together for you, mentally at least, and you will have a glimpse of what these ideas can produce, where they can take you. For sure, money matters will come up for you to take care of. Be business-like in resolving any issues but do not allow this to overshadow the good that can be accomplished this month.

Your time may be taken up with new agendas, but avoid rushing things now as the energy of the Nine PYC is still in force. Be prepared for new places and meeting new people, forming new associations. The new idea or proposal that comes to you will be something out of the ordinary. Consider it, even though you realise that it may take time to materialise. Understand that the High-End demands for demonstrating compassion, understanding and forgiveness are still operating. Life is intent on elevating your good character and spiritual consciousness. Creative thinking is what will begin the build towards what you want in your future. October might ask that you stand your ground on some issue – do so with a quiet confidence, as someone who knows. Be assertive in your responses, but avoid anything stronger. Accept that you need others, that they can help you, so it's important that you cooperate as necessary. Take charge of your life, but do not exclude others. Keep your health in top form and do not allow the little things to get the better of you. Play it right and you could be in for a pleasant surprise.

Your best responses for October
- Accept the help that is offered to you.
- Take note of how and to where your finances are moving.
- Be more business responsive.
- In your decisions, use logic more and emotion less.
- Use the courage and foresight October offers to gauge future potential.

November in a NINE Personal Year Cycle

November gears up to be a busy month with lots in your diary. It's certainly not a time to hide from the world, but a time to direct your light to where it can shine brightest. You may feel a pull that is more introspective, but do not allow yourself to go too deep within. If any thoughts or memories crowd in that are less than positive, be sure to bless them and release them into the past, back to the state of what was and is no more. Utilise your time collecting data and information in regards to the ideas and plans that you have been working on. Part of November's energy supports the help that others can give, so do not feel that it's all up to you, do not be bashful in asking friends and associates for help.

In a month which offers a chance to master opposing energies, perhaps someone may overstep their mark in trying to persuade you to act against your convictions. They may even contribute to the problem. In all this, take care to not allow feelings of negative sensitivity to creep in now. Resolve any problems with the application of tact and diplomacy; combine authority with gentleness in your approach. Be particularly vigilant in these qualities when your patience starts to wear thin. Feelings of resentment may try to muscle in, but only if you give them space. It's natural to feel anxious as you wait for things to improve. Remind yourself that just because you cannot see the final outcome yet does not mean that things are not working out as you planned. Give yourself a massive injection of faith and cooperate with those who are with you on this. Your health and the health of others may need to be considered this month. Enjoy the social aspect so much a part of November.

Your best responses for November
- Showcase an authority tempered with diplomacy.
- Observe the situation before making your move.
- Avoid taking the lead when the better option may be cooperation.
- Refuse to give negative thoughts or motives any oxygen.
- Be more selective in what you share and with whom you share it.

December in a NINE Personal Year Cycle

December's energy encourages you to spend a little more time and money on yourself, to be kind to yourself and to factor in experiences that make you happy. Maybe you can catch up with a friend or two over lunch or pencil in something else that makes your heart sing. Entertaining and the purchase of Christmas gifts for you and those you love will keep you busy. Though you can afford to loosen your purse-strings a little, remember to keep any hint of extravagance carried in December's energy within your credit limit. Self-expression and inspiration bring rewards. Thoughtful communication is key to making good impressions. Make sure what you say is what you mean. The opportunity for career advancement along creative lines is a real possibility.

And yet in all this you will sense that something is different. You may feel that this is not your usual December experience. With a combination of so many emotional numbers in this month's energy field, you will experience both joy and sadness pulling at your heartstrings. Life brings you experiences to show you care, along with a fair share of responsibility. It's a busy month that will have you wondering if it's at all possible for you to accomplish all that you want to do as well as all that is expected of you. There is no need for concern, rest assured that you will, even if at times it can feel overwhelming. Your mind may be guilty of bringing forth some bittersweet moments, though December's intention is to encourage you to be more happy and optimistic than anything else. In all this, there are celebrations to be enjoyed with family and friends. December offers you a chance to inspire others – by the way you communicate your words and the way you express your feelings. By the love and care you give those in need. A chance to shine your light ever so brightly.

Your best responses for December
- Respond to family matters with love and care.
- Responsibilities may feel heavy, just do your best.
- Celebrate the good and the beautiful, leave anything less out the door.
- Express your feelings with grace.
- Be in awe of Life's wonder and beauty and your part in it – Be an expression of that!

Closing Thoughts

Many of you may remember a song John Denver made famous – 'Some Days are Diamonds, Some Days are Stone'. There's an honest truth in these words which we cannot deny. And in our humanity, when we are happy, we want that feeling to last forever. We want time to stand still. When we are going through the tough stuff, we want to hurry time along. We want it to pass quickly. Life really is a combination of diamonds and stone, as the song reminds us.

Sometimes we falsely believe that some people 'have it easy'. But is this true? I think not. We all have our challenges, even if what is challenging for me might be a breeze-through for you, and vice versa.

I encourage you to use your stone days to build, to store, to carry, to cut and to carve. Use them as life-building blocks. And your diamond days? Compliment yourself on your build, of course. And then, relish and enjoy every facet of those diamonds. Be in awe of every sparkle. Be grateful that they made it through the tough stuff. For surviving the dark nights, the digs, the cuts, the buffs and polishes. Admire their beauty, praise their value, and be grateful, be humbly grateful, for they too were once stone.

May you live a rich and meaningful life …

Anna B.